PASTOR FROM GAZA

Hanna Massad

ISBN: 0692137769
ISBN-13: 978-0692137765

Unless otherwise noted, all Scripture references are from the New International Version of the Bible.

Scripture taken from the Holy Bible, NEW INTERNATIONAL VERSION®, NIV® Copyright © 1973, 1978, 1984, 2011 by Biblica, Inc.® Used by permission. All rights reserved worldwide.

Scripture quotations marked TPT are from The Passion Translation®, Copyright ©2017 by BroadStreet Publishing® Group, LLC. Used by permission. All rights reserved, thePassionTranslation.com.

Scripture quotations taken from the New American Standard Bible® (NASB), Copyright © 1960, 1962, 1963, 1968, 1971, 1972, 1973,v1975, 1977, 1995 by The Lockman Foundation. Used by permission. www.Lockman.org

CMG
publishing

To my parents, George and Mimi
and my siblings Salem, Rita, Renee, Mona and Mai,
who inspired me with their patience and love.

To my wife, Suhad,
who walked with me
in the midst of the fires of persecution,
and to our daughters, Joyce and Jolene,
who also have suffered for just being daughters
of a Palestinian pastor from Gaza.

HANNA MASSAD HAS LIVED THROUGH MORE DANGER THAN MOST PEOPLE HAVE SEEN ON TV.

It's not strange to see a Baptist church in Israel, or in the West Bank for that matter, but try pastoring one in the Gaza Strip. While Hanna lived in Gaza as the only evangelical pastor in the Strip, he shepherded the small flock of believers during both the first Palestinian Intifada, which began in 1987, and the second Palestinian Intifada, which launched in 2000.

In a thrilling new read, Hanna Massad takes you deep into the heart of the Strip and uncovers what life is like for an endangered species in Gaza-Palestinian Christians. The risk of death that believers endure daily in the 6 mile wide-26 mile long strip is enormous as they are caught in between the ongoing battles between Hamas and Israel. Hanna has faced personal threat, member of his church have been martyred, and he has suffered personal losses that are unimaginable.

But he remains humble, godly example of everything that Jesus taught and lived during His earthly life. I could not put this book down and I whole-heartedly recommend it to you. You have brothers and sisters in the Gaza Strip that love Jesus with their whole heart. Get to know them and the man of God that was their shepherd so many years and the power of Christ that resonates through him. Thank you Hanna for risking your life to follow Jesus and being God's man in Gaza.

Tom Doyle
President, *UnCharted Ministries*

(Tom Doyle is author of *Dreams and Visions Is Jesus Awakening the Muslim World?* and *Standing in the Fire.*)

Contents

Introduction

A STRATEGIC MEDITERRANEAN PORT along the ancient caravan route between Egypt and Syria, my hometown was once populated by giants—the offspring of angels who married the daughters of men.[1] Napoleon would one day describe Gaza as "the outpost of Africa, the door to Asia."[2]

For several centuries, Egyptians ruled Canaan, referring to my hometown as Ghazzat, *a prized city.*

Armies of chariots and 10,000 foot-soldiers under the pharaoh Thutmose III thundered through Gaza and defeated a coalition of Canaanite chiefdoms at Megiddo in 1458 BC. The Egyptians then built fortresses, mansions, and agricultural estates from Gaza to Galilee...[3]

Samson, judge and deliverer of Israel—blinded and bound with bronze—brought down the temple of Dagon and killed three thousand Philistines in my hometown.[4]

By the 15th century AD, Arab traders had settled in Gaza. Chief among them was Umar ibn al-Khattab, who would become one of Islam's most powerful caliphs.

Muhammad's great-grandfather is believed to be buried under the dome of Gaza's Sayed al-Hashim Mosque.

---

[1] Genesis 6:1-4; Numbers 13:33; Joshua 11:22.
[2] *Guerre dans I' Orient: Cam- pagnes d' Egypte el de Syrie*, par Napoleon lui-m6me, ii., ch. 7.
[3] Atwood, Roger, "Egypt's Final Redoubt in Canaan," *Archaeology*: a publication of the Archaelogical Institute of America, 12 June 2017.
[4] Judges 16:21-31.

As the Muslim Arab population grew, religious leaders turned churches into mosques, imposed oppressive taxes on Christians and Jews, established Islam as the official religion and decreed Arabic to be the common language.

Throughout the centuries, scores of banners have flown over Gaza—from Rome's SPQR and the Ottoman star and crescent to the Union Jack and Tricolour. Scores of gods have been worshipped there, including bloodthirsty Baal, son of Dagon, and more recently the deadly Spirit of Nationalism.

But neither kings and caliphs nor idols of gold and clay can stand against God's plan to redeem mankind through the birth, death and resurrection of His Son, Jesus, the Christ—a cosmic drama that began within walking distance of my hometown.

Today, Gaza is about the size of Las Vegas, with an average of nearly 13,000 people packed into every square mile, making it one of the most densely populated pieces of real estate on Earth. As I write this, nearly half the population is under fourteen years of age. Only three out of a hundred live past sixty-five.

As a result of a ten-year siege by Israel, less than five percent of the water is fit to drink, with seawater, sewage and chemicals contaminating Gaza's overloaded aquifer. Electricity is available for about four hours a day. Unemployment is forty-four percent, and three out of ten Palestinians live below the $1.90-a-day poverty line, leaving Gaza totally dependent upon foreign humanitarian aid. Unless steps are taken to address this economic and humanitarian crisis, the UN warns, Gaza will be uninhabitable by 2020.

My thoughts are often about injustice because I am Palestinian and it is in the air I breathe. In my experience, injustice is even more devastating than violence, because it cuts through flesh, deep into soul and spirit.

It seemed that just about everywhere I went growing up in Gaza—through checkpoints and border crossings, in the streets during the Occupation—I was yelled at and harassed, just for being Palestinian.

The voices still echo in my head, stimulating the part of my brain that controls my emotions, making my muscles tense, increasing the stress hormones in my blood, triggering fear. And the images in my head never fade, refreshed by a headline, old wounds reopened with every step through the ancient streets of my hometown.

But a servant is not greater than his master. Jesus was humiliated and executed for crimes and sins He did not commit and even forsaken by His Father who He had never disobeyed.

The scourging and crucifixion were horrible. But the injustice broke Him and made Him cry out, "Why?"[5]

---

[5] Matthew 27:46.

1. Growing up

Palestinian

IT WAS TOO HOT and too noisy to sleep. The few fans mounted on the walls provided little relief against the sweltering heat of summer in the Middle East. Sweaty, overtired children and babies whined and cried as they tried to find comfortable positions on the concrete floor or atop a parent's luggage.

Several hundred men, women and children were crammed into a small hall designed to hold two hundred—people visiting or returning to their families in Gaza, people in wheelchairs, old people, sick people coming home after treatment or hospitalization, businessmen, students, laborers.

I had just returned from America after being fingerprinted for my citizenship application and was stranded on the Egyptian side of the Rafah Crossing, one of only two ways in or out of Gaza, the other being the northern Erez Crossing into Israel.

My name was confusing for Americans. Hanna is Arabic for John. But in the United States, it is a girl's name. And so I would get mail addressed to Miss or Mrs. Hanna Massad. One day, I received an invitation to a conference and they said "we know the pain you are going through as the wife of a pastor. This conference was made especially for you." I didn't go. People still confuse me with my wife.

The air churned with angry voices. Husbands and wives blamed each other, while Palestinians blamed the Egyptians, Israelis, Hamas or the Palestinian Authority

(PA), or they just blamed the West. Police barked instructions, maybe out of frustration, maybe in an attempt to intimidate and maintain order. Yelling. Always yelling.

One time, when I was crossing through Rafah, I tried to take pictures of the terrible conditions. An officer saw me and took me to an area where he began to scream at me.

"This is a restricted area!" he shouted. "Pictures are forbidden!"

He glared at me as he made certain that I deleted all the pictures, despite the fact that I had never seen any sign that the hall was a restricted area or that banned photography.

Inside the waiting hall, even the people who checked our documents and luggage were harsh and hard to deal with. They had no computers, so everything was written by hand, which added to delays and increased frustrations.

I had been stuck there for three days and nights, filling the endless hours with prayer, reading and calls to my wife, trying to sleep at night on top of a wooden box used by customs officers to inspect luggage. I dreaded the thought of another night there. A friend of mine had been stuck at the crossing for ten days, another for six weeks. It is common for thousands of travelers, victims of politics or recent events, to be stranded on one side of the gate or the other, spilling out of cramped waiting areas and spread out over scorching pavement or sand, waiting for days or weeks before being permitted to pass through to the other side.

Some sick people get sicker. Some pregnant women give birth or miscarry. Sometimes, people die waiting. Young people gather together and manage to turn an ordeal into a social event, their loud music blaring and jarring frazzled nerves, even from the fringes of the crowd.

Favoritism makes things even worse. You don't take a number or have a place in line. If you are outside, you may be in the midst of a crowd that seems to spread out forever. Suddenly, the gate opens to let an individual or a group or a hundred people pass through, while all the rest are pushed back. How? Why? Because they know people in the PA or bribed someone. It's not fair, but that's how it works.

Once, when my wife and I were taking our newborn daughter to meet her grandparents in Jordan, we were among the favored. We had left home at 8 am and been waiting in the suffocating heat all day, Joyce in Suhad's arms. Around midnight, we saw a PA border guard we knew from the Christian community. I think he took pity on us because of Joyce.

Someone helped us throw our luggage over the high fence, and the guard opened the gate just enough for us to squeeze through. The crowd rushed the gate as it slammed shut again. It all happened so fast that the heavy gate nearly hit Joyce in the head. But Suhad shielded her, and the gate hit her arm so hard that it hurt for weeks. I can't imagine the damage it might have done to our infant daughter.

Today, though, I had no one to help me. I had nothing but endless hours to pray, think and remember.

My mother was born in Jaffa, near Tel Aviv. In 1948, during the Arab-Israeli War, she and her family were among 700,000 Palestinians driven from their homes by IDF[6] soldiers. Shortly after the war, the Israelis conducted a 24-hour census of the captured area and decreed that none of the Palestinians who were absent from their land that day could return to their homes. My father's family lost seventeen acres near Ashkelon, about thirty miles south of Tel Aviv and eight miles north of the Gaza border. We still have the title documents.

---

[6] Israeli Defense Forces.

Palestinian children grow up in Gaza and the West Bank hearing the stories from their parents and grandparents of how the Israelis took their homes and their land. When they leave for school in the morning, many pass keys hanging on the doorpost, keys to the home their family lost, relentless reminders of the injustice. Later, in history class, they hear it all over again.

Little wonder that wounds and bitterness pass from generation to generation, each generation trying to get back what ancestors lost.

My parents' first child was a son, Salem, followed by four girls—Rita, Renee, Mona and Mai. Sadly, a hereditary form of Muscular Dystrophy ran in our family. It attacked all the children except one of the girls. One day, it would also claim my mother's life.

There are several kinds of Muscular Dystrophy. Ours was Myotonic, also known as Steinert's Disease, which manifests in an inability to voluntarily relax the muscles of the face, neck, fingers and ankles. There is no cure.

People felt uncomfortable when they passed them in the streets, seeing the effects of the disease in the muscles of their faces and the limp in their walk. As a result, my brother and sisters were not openly accepted in the Palestinian community. Even my parents had trouble coming to terms with the disease. My mother insisted that there was no disease, that the symptoms were the result of a fall when she was pregnant.

Sons are highly valued in Middle Eastern culture, and my father was desperate for another boy.

"If I get a boy," he promised God, "I will sacrifice a lamb."

I was born in 1960.[7]

---

[7] My father was too poor to buy a lamb when his prayer was answered. When I was 16, someone gave me a gift, and I used it to buy a lamb so my father could fulfil his vow.

My father was well-educated and fluent in English. He worked in communications for the Egyptians who ruled Gaza at that time. We lived in a house in downtown Gaza City with my uncle and his family. It was an old building. My uncle's family had one room and we had two, one downstairs and one upstairs. Extended families traditionally live together in the Middle East.

When I was six, my uncle Issa went to Egypt to study to be a journalist. Once, when he came back to Gaza, he brought me a bicycle. I remember this very well, because he was a student, and he paid for it out of the little money he had and carried it all the way back on the train. The following year, in June 1967, another uncle, Yousef, fought against the Israelis. Less than a week after it started, Israel conquered the Sinai and seized East Jerusalem, the West Bank and the Golan Heights. Then, when my uncle returned to Gaza, the Israelis arrested and tortured him, which affected him mentally for the rest of his life.

I want to make it clear before I go on that I describe Israel's injustices against the Palestinian people only as points of fact. I love the Jewish people, even though I have suffered at their hands, just as I love the Palestinian people and the Egyptians, in spite of the persecution and their abuses against us.

I remember one day, during the first Gulf War in 1990, going upstairs to seal the all the windows against Saddam's chemical weapons. I felt horrible about this war. I am against wars and people killing each other, regardless of their ethnicity or their background. When I looked at my father, he seemed to be torn between the pain of past injustices and the thought of missiles being fired into civilian populations in Israel. Nevertheless, he was shocked when I expressed my love for the Jewish people, because they are created in the image of God, as is the rest of humanity.

God put love in my heart for everybody. I could never love them in my own strength. The pain is too deep and the offenses too many and too frequent. I am able to love everyone because I experience constantly the love of Jesus, and I can forgive much because God has forgiven so much in me. So I hope you won't hear bitterness or offense in my narrative where I am trying only to express pain. Pain is inevitable with offense. What is important is our response to it, whether with love and forgiveness or with unforgiveness and hatred.

My father lost his job after Israel won the war. Struggling to support his family, he opened a clothing shop. It did not do very well. I remember at the end of the day my mother would ask him how much he sold, and sometimes it was nothing.

During the Israeli Occupation that followed the war, my father got a job with the Israeli Ministry of Interior, dealing with business taxes, but he still struggled to make ends meet. While he worked for the Israelis, his boss tried to get him to collaborate with them. I learned about this much later. He refused, but he ended up with high blood pressure, because we all knew that even suspected Israeli collaborators had been killed. The PLO[8] one time suspected our nextdoor neighbor, who was a policeman, of being a collaborator. During Ramadan, they came to his house, took him away and killed him.

Not all who were suspected actually turned out to be collaborators. Some were reported by people who saw an opportunity to settle old scores or who stood to gain from their deaths.

Around this time, the Egyptian government enabled my father to buy a piece of land at a cheap price, though it would take ten years and many loans in order to finish a house on it. A Bedouin family lived on our land with their tents and flock and protected the property while our house was being built. I remember going with their children to shepherd their sheep.

---

[8] The Palestine Liberation Organization was a resistance movement, led by Yasser Arafat, that claimed to represent the Palestinian people and that morphed into today's Palestinian Authority.

In 1968, though it wasn't completed, we moved in. Even the roads around us were incomplete. Few were paved. Most were just trails through deep sand.

Sand was everywhere. Part of the floor of our house was still sand. But I didn't care. We were close to the beautiful blue Mediterranean, and the air was filled with the breath of the sea, which lifted my kite as I flew it from the roof.

In addition to the delicious salty air, I remember the smell of fresh baked bread. Every other evening, my mother mixed dough, leavened it and cut it into twenty pieces, one piece per loaf. The next morning, she put the pieces on a special wooden board, and I carried it on my head about a mile to the public bakery.[9] My mother's cooking was the aroma of heaven on earth to me. I loved her stuffed chicken with special rice, young doves and soup with her special meatballs. Mostly, however, we could only afford fried potatoes, eggplant and rice. Once
or twice a week, we had meat. We also raised some of our own food—chickens in a corner of our property and doves, a special favorite in the Middle East.

A couple times, when I was ten years old, I stole some eggs, sold them and kept the money. Once, though, I hid the eggs in the sand. My family discovered them, rebuked me and ended my crime spree.

My father did his best. His paycheck was always gone after the first week and he would have to borrow money to feed us for the rest of the month. The next payday, he would pay off his debt and the cycle would begin again.

---

[9] Eventually, people got ovens in their homes, and now the public bakeries sell their own pita and other breads and pastries.

When I was in the fourth grade, I looked out of the classroom window one day during break and saw a military vehicle filled with what we referred to as "red hats."[10] They were really scary. They dragged a bunch of young Palestinian men from the vehicle, shoved them up against a wall and beat them with truncheons.

I saw more of them once when I was with my father at the market. We hid because the red hats could stop anyone in the street any time they wanted and do whatever they wanted, as they did to the demonstrators who suffered the inevitable Israeli backlash.

One day, listening to PLO Radio, I heard about some *fedayeen,* (PLO members) killed by the IDF. Gaza's largest hospital was next to our elementary school, so my friends and I went nextdoor to see the bodies. They were lying in the shade of a big tree. All of them were in their twenties. Despite our curiosity, the sight terrified us. Mostly though, I remember the sadness of their families and friends who came to mourn and to show their respect.

As I grew older and realized how hard my father struggled to provide for his family, I began to look for ways to help out. When I was ten, I went into business with a neighbor. We made popcorn at his house and sold it in the streets. After sixth grade, and for the next several years during summer holidays, I worked for a Jewish carpenter, building food and vegetable crates out of wood and wire.

Of course, it wasn't all work. I loved soccer, and I told my father I really wanted to buy a soccer ball with some of the money I had earned. He said no, because it was too expensive. But I bought it anyway. It cost 25 Israeli lira.[11]

---

[10] Maroon berets were worn by Israeli troops of the Tzanhanim Airborne Brigade and elite special forces units.

[11] The Israeli pound, or Israeli lira, was the currency of the State of Israel from 9 June 1952 until 23 February 1980, when it was replaced with the shekel on 24 February 1980, which was again replaced with the New Shekel in 1985.

18

One day, I was walking home and ran into my father sitting with some men on a bench outside the supermarket. When he saw the new soccer ball, he left the gathering and followed me to our house and started to hit me with his sandals because I had disrespected him, and he insisted that I return it.

My mother felt sorry for me and asked her wealthy sister, who was living in Brazil, if she could send us a soccer ball. She didn't do it behind my father's back or anything like that, and he let me keep this one because it was "free" and because I think he felt bad about what had happened.

I also loved to swim, though I wasn't a great swimmer, and I loved the Mediterranean. When I was about fourteen, I walked down to the beach one afternoon for a swim. I didn't have any money to put my clothes in a safe place, so I left them on the beach. The swim was wonderful. But when I came out of the water, my pants were gone. Though I had lost a pair of good pants, my family got a big laugh out of it and enjoyed sharing the story with others, especially after I had become a pastor.

But I'm getting ahead of myself.

At fifteen, I got my first job in Israel. I went to the eastern border where a Palestinian contractor felt our muscles to see if we were strong enough. Those who were judged fit were put into a big truck, like a military troop transport with benches in the back.

For hours, we worked in the sun, bent over, picking onions, sunflowers, watermelons or tomatoes. The contractor was abusive, swearing at us and coming after us with his belt to make us work faster. But the money was good. I did this for several years, and my family began to feel the effect of my help.

Hiring out as day labor was risky. You never knew what might happen. One day, I worked for an Israeli Bedouin all day. At the end of the day, he picked us up to take us back to Gaza.

"Okay," he said, "wait here a minute while I turn the car around." That was the last we saw of him.

Tens of thousands of Palestinians crossed the borders every day to work in Israel, so I had to get up at 3:30 in the morning in order to arrive early enough to find a good-paying job for the day. When I was sixteen or seventeen, I worked in a juice factory, near the city of Rehovet. After I worked there for eight or nine hours, I went on to a second job where we filled trucks with fruits and vegetables. Sometimes, I worked 24 hours at a time.

I remember one day, after working a long stretch, I went to a corner at about 3 am to take a nap. But the supervisor told me to keep working. I was supposed to operate heavy equipment that moved material around on a high cement stage. The machine went out of control, and I fell and slashed one of my toes. Without medical insurance, the hospital only cleaned me up and sent me home. Fortunately, my father took me to a relative who was a doctor. The nail on that toe is still different, even after more than forty years.

I also had good experiences with Israelis.

One morning, a Muslim neighbor and I decided to go to the beach. We took a taxi to Ashkelon but, instead of boarding the bus to the beach, we mistakenly got on the bus to Tel Aviv, thirty miles to the north. We also had different tickets. His would take him back to Ashkelon. Mine only allowed me to travel in and around Tel Aviv. So the Arab driver made me get off.

To show you the heart of the Jewish people, when several of them saw what happened, they went over to the driver and gave him the money for me to get home.

I have always remembered that kindness.

2. Light in the Sand

MY FAMILY WAS GREEK ORTHODOX. And though we were Christians, we were influenced by the Islamic culture around us, like the way women should dress and how men and women should relate to one another. In school, we learned Islamic history and the teachings of the Qur'an. All of our neighbors were Muslim, so most of my friends were, too. Mostly, it wasn't a problem. Sometimes, though, our religions clashed.

When I was ten, one neighbor would make the sign of the cross and spit on it, because this is what he was taught by his family. And sometimes kids would curse me and blaspheme, which hurt me and made me feel different, like I didn't belong. But I think God used the Islamic influence to draw me to him.

Growing up, I never experienced a personal relationship with the Lord in the Greek Orthodox Church. But there was a mosque a couple hundred yards from our home. So, five times every day, we heard the call to prayer. I thought, if there was a true religion on the earth, it must be Islam because of the Muslims' dedication. I watched my friends wake up early every morning to pray, then pray four more times throughout the day. It created a hunger in me that eventually was satisfied when my born-again aunt led me to the only evangelical church in Gaza. Though Aunt Salema had not finished elementary school and could barely read and write, she taught me how to pray and study the Bible. She had a wonderful testimony, even from Muslims, how
she lived her life, how humble, loving and kind she was.

In the summer of 1975, when I was fifteen, Aunt Salema invited me to attend a youth meeting. I was amazed because I had never heard the Gospel presented so simply and clearly. My heart was wide open. I never realized before that we have such a treasure in the Bible and in the person of Jesus. It touched my heart deeply, and I began to experience God's forgiveness, love and peace.

My heart changed completely. I could not get enough of God. I wanted to read the Bible all the time. I wanted to sing all the time, to the point that I think my family got tired of me. I felt as though I was flying, and God sent wonderful mentors to disciple, love and direct me.

I never imagined then that I would one day serve as the pastor of that church.

To be a Christian in Palestine means to be a member of a traditional church like Saint Porphyrius, which dates back to 425 AD and was rebuilt by the Crusaders in the 12th century. Leaving that church was perceived as a bad insult to the entire Greek Orthodox community. So my move to a Baptist church made it hard on my family. They were okay with it in the beginning because they thought it would keep me from going wild as a teenager. Then, I told them I wanted to be baptized.

"You are already baptized!" my father said. "What are you talking about?"

He was very angry because my being baptized as an adult made him look weak in front of the community. They would see it as his son disrespecting him. But I was desperate because the church policy at that time was that, unless you were baptized as an adult, you were not supposed to receive communion, and I really wanted to
take communion. Nevertheless, while I lived under my father's roof, I would respect his wishes.

One day, however, I talked with three other young believers who were not baptized, and we decided to take communion on our own. We climbed into the church through a window, prayed for three hours and then solemnly gave one another the bread and grape juice. That's how hungry we were. To us, it was like being in heaven.[12]

A year later, I approached my father again.

"Okay," he said, "you can be baptized. But not in Gaza."

So I went to Ramallah in the West Bank with some other Christians to be baptized.

In Palestine, the final exam in high school was very difficult and determined a great deal of a person's future. There was great pressure to excel. So I spent all my time studying and stopped going to church.

After I graduated, I never seemed to get around to going back, and for a couple of years I just drifted.

My father wanted to send me to study in Syria, but when he went to check it out, undercover police followed him everywhere he went. So he was afraid to send me into that kind of environment. The PLO offered scholarships, but my family thought it would be dangerous for me to place myself under obligation to them.

Meanwhile, Aunt Salema never stopped praying for me and encouraging me to go back to church, and finally her persistence paid off.

In 1980, A Lebanese evangelist named Maurice Gerges, known as "the Billy Graham of the Middle East," came to Gaza. I was so convicted that I couldn't wait until he finished preaching. I went to the front in tears. The years of poverty and need, the oppression and rejection, the dangers and hardships suddenly seemed like nothing at all. I no longer felt alone and knew that I would never be lonely again.

---

[12] Given the difficulties that many faced in being baptized as adults, the church eventually changed its policy, not wanting anyone to be deprived of partaking in the Lord's Supper.

For the next few years I went to school at the Baptist hospital, studying to become a lab technician.

A Baptist facility since 1954, the hospital and its nursing school were turned over to the Anglicans in 1982. I worked there until 1987, loved, embraced and discipled by Jim MacPherson, Jack Hodges and others and sharing the love and mercy of Christ with hundreds of Muslims and other hospital staff in chapel.[13]

Sometimes we were able to go into Israel to the house of an American missionary to worship and study the Bible with Jewish believers—evidence that the animosity and hatred between Palestinians and Jews is neither inherent nor inevitable.

We worked long hours in the laboratory, sometimes thirty-six hours straight. At night, when things quieted down, I listened to taped sermons and Christian music. I felt very close to the Lord among the slides and test-tubes. One night, I was asked to draw blood from a man from a refugee camp in the south of Gaza. The propane tank in his kitchen had exploded, and he had suffered critical burns.

He was still awake when I arrived and, as soon as he realized that I was a Christian, he was very excited. He was a Muslim-background believer who had been led to Christ while listening to Christian radio. After he became a Christian, people thought he was crazy. He spoke passionately about his love for Jesus and asked if I could get him a cross and ask a pastor to come to him. It was late, but I told him I would see what I could do.

At 3 am, the cardiac arrest signal went off. Doctors, nurses and lab workers rushed to his room. But he had gone to be with the Lord. God finds us, no matter where we are, even in the forgotten refugee camps of Gaza.

---

[13] Most staff members were Muslims, who attended chapel because it was mandatory.

In 1986, I was invited to attend the International Conference for Itinerant Evangelists in Amsterdam. Except for working in Israel, I had never been out of Palestine. What a joy and privilege to be among 8,000 traveling evangelists from 180 nations for a week and a half! The media called it "the largest gathering ever held solely for those on the front lines of the Gospel."[14]

When I arrived, I found an invitation in my welcome bag to sit on the stage with Billy Graham. I was shy to sit by one of the greatest men of God in the world, embarrassed at the end of the meeting to go shake his hand and once again amazed at our Father's goodness.

Year after year, my hunger for God and understanding of his Word continued to grow. Scripture was like bread to me. No, it was more like cake, not just
nourishing but delicious. Even when I felt full, it wasn't enough, and as soon as I stopped eating, I was hungry for more. I was like a child at a birthday party.

I decided to go to Bible college in America. When my father found my application, he tore it up because

he thought pastors were just people who passed a plate and collected money. In time, though, he realized I was serious about my faith and became more open.

Gaza Baptist Church had never been led by a local pastor, just visiting or temporary pastors from Egypt or Lebanon who came, stayed a year or two and returned home, except for Egyptian pastor Hanna Ibrahim, who stayed 15 years. As I watched them come and go, God began to give me a vision to serve his children in Gaza.

I shared my heart with a few people and, in 1987, I was invited by the church where God had changed my life to serve as their first Palestinian pastor.

---

[14] Davis, James D., Religion Editor, *SunSentinel*, 12 July 1986.

When the Greek Orthodox heard the news, a priest came to our house to persuade my father not to allow my ordination. He told him that Protestants, especially Evangelicals, disrespect Mary and that sort of thing. He didn't succeed, and my father didn't tell me at the time because he didn't want it to trouble me. My parents attended my ordination on October 18, 1987, along with pastors from the West Bank and missionaries from Israel.

Back then, the congregation of Gaza Baptist Church numbered only about twenty people, though as many as sixty usually attended services, including Catholic, Greek Orthodox and Muslims. Only a score were baptized. Those who came from other churches were afraid to be baptized because of the effect it would have on their families and communities.

The Muslims came to listen, curious and hungry for truth. Some eventually became believers, but at a very dear price. When the father of one new Christian found out, he tried to shoot his son while he slept. Somehow, he missed. The family of another convert reported him
and accused him of being an Israeli collaborator, and he was put in prison.

One time, two Muslim men knocked at the front door of our home and began threatening me and my family. The sister of one of the men who used to attend our church had disappeared, and they demanded that we tell them where she was. When I explained that we knew nothing about her disappearance, they threatened to turn militant groups against us. Another family member called and threatened us over the phone. Eventually, the girl returned home and the threats ended. This was very difficult for my family, especially my father.

Being a pastor was more difficult than I had anticipated, partly because the congregation was so small that I struggled financially and partly because they had known me since I was a child. They knew my family and about our disease, and all of this affected their attitude toward me. Also, I was a single man of twenty-seven, naïve and inexperienced.

I took classes at Bethlehem Bible College (BBC) to improve myself. And Aunt Salma continued to be a faithful supporter and encourager. On Sundays, after church, I usually went over to her house, where she refilled my hungry spirit as well as my growling stomach.

In 1991, I had an opportunity to get married.

Financially, I was barely getting by. How would I take care of a wife and family? Besides, all I wanted was to dig deeper and deeper into God's Word. In America, I could immerse myself in it, in addition to getting the education and training I needed to become a more effective pastor. I had no peace about settling down and decided to leave.

"Who will take care of your brother and sisters?" my father asked. "You are the healthy one."

Eventually, he agreed to give me his blessing, as long as I promised to come back to Gaza after I finished college. I agreed, and he called my uncle to come over to be a witness.

3. America

I LANDED IN LOS ANGELES September 18, 1991 and took a taxi to Fuller Theological Seminary in Pasadena.

Established in 1947, Fuller has about 3,000 students from nearly 100 nations and nearly every denomination.[15] It offers three schools: Theology, Psychology and Intercultural Studies. I chose Theology.

On Christmas eve, three months after I arrived,[16] my father died. I was devastated that I hadn't been there and that I didn't have enough money to return for his funeral. At that time, Occupied Gaza[17] was in turmoil over family reunification issues, and I was afraid I might not be permitted to leave again.

The $2,000 I had in my pocket when I arrived didn't go very far in Southern California.[18] But God is always faithful.

In the Fall, Jews for Jesus founder Moshe Rosen invited me to speak at a conference in San Francisco. We had met in 1989 during a prayer meeting at the Lausanne II International Congress on World Evangelization in the Philippines and had kept in touch.

Several hundred people were in attendance, many of whom were Messianic Jews. After I shared my heart, Moshe encouraged people to give to help me in my studies.

---

[15] Fuller alumni include authors Richard Foster, John Piper, C. Peter Wagner, Michael Youssef, David Stern and Rick Warren, as well as Campus Crusade founder Bill Bright, leading theologians and media leaders.

[16] Greek Orthodox Christmas is January 7.

[17] My use of the term "Occupied Gaza" is intended as a historical reference, rather than a political term, to distinguish Gaza between 1967 and 2005 from Gaza prior to the Six-Day War and after Israel's disengagement from Gaza and North Sinai.

[18] My retirement money when I resigned from Gaza Baptist Church. Financial aid covered most of my tuition and board at Fuller.

While I sat there, one of the leaders came up to me very excited and told me the response was amazing. I left with a very generous donation, sufficient to support me for several months. Later, another Messianic believer helped me buy a motorcycle.

Isn't it just like God to touch the hearts of a roomful of Jewish believers to bless a Palestinian kid from Gaza?

I did what I could to stretch my finances, in order to be able to regularly send some money back to my family. For a year and a half, I cleaned cages at a veterinary clinic for a small salary and a room. It took me about a week to be able to sleep with all the barking and meowing . . . and the smell.

One day, a friend introduced me to a wonderful couple named George and Anita Brandow, who lived in San Marino. He had been staying with them but was graduating and I was invited to take his place.

George Brandow was a structural engineer whose Sports Arena, Convention Center and Central Library helped shape the Los Angeles skyline. In exchange for room and board, I took care of their two dogs. They even gave me money every month, which enabled me to send some to my family.

I never forgot my first night there. We were sitting on the porch of that beautiful house, eating dinner, surrounded by a beautiful lawn and garden. I told them I felt like I had just moved from Hell to Heaven. I lived there for six years, during which time I completed my master's degree work and continued on into the doctoral program.

My life at Fuller was hectic. I took sixteen credit hours per quarter while working multiple jobs. One summer, I took twenty hours. I wouldn't have made it without my private time with God. Even Jesus "often withdrew to lonely places and prayed."[19]

---

[19] Luke 5:16.

One of my favorite "lonely places" was in a tiny chapel inside the library. Another was Fuller's prayer garden, with its stone benches and waterfall. There was something calming about moving water that helped me connect with God. Maybe that's why Jesus spent so much time alone with His Father beside the Sea of Galilee.

In 1994, two weeks after my Aunt Salma died of cancer, I returned home for the first time, heartbroken that I had been absent when another person so close to my heart had passed away. I walked through the house and looked in all the rooms filled with memories of my father, and I wept.

My mother tried to comfort me, and I asked her if my father was happy with me when he died. She said yes, he was happy that I had not forgotten him and proud that I was sending money for the family.

I stayed about a month, during which time, a missionary approached me and asked me to pastor Gaza Baptist Church again. But I felt it wasn't time yet and returned to Pasadena.

While working on my master's degree, I served a nine-month internship with First Baptist Church of Pasadena, during which time I applied for my green card.
But by the time the interview came for the green card, I had finished the internship.

"Are you still working with the Baptist church?" the USCIS[20] officer asked.

"No, I already completed my internship."

"I'm sorry, but I cannot give you a green card."

"But I was honest with you."

"Thank you for being honest, but I cannot help you because the internship is over, right?"

"So what happens now, because my student visa has expired."

---

[20] US Citizenship and Immigration Services.

31

At that time, I had been talking to the board at First Baptist Church of Azuza about working for them.

"If they agree," the officer said, "we can proceed with your green card application."

A month later, I became pastor of First Baptist Church of Azuza, established in 1875. This was another example of God's faithfulness, as well as his sense of humor—a Palestinian Christian with developing English skills and a thick Arabic accent pastoring a Caucasian church in Azusa, California.

Like Gaza Baptist Church, the 40-member congregation of Azusa Baptist was dwarfed in its 350-seat sanctuary. But this tiny flock still holds a big place in my heart. I remember the wonderful times when, after filling our spirits with God's Word, we headed down to the local Taco Bell to fill our bellies.

What opposites we were! I was thirty-six years old; most of them were elderly. Some were in their 90s and unable to come on Sundays, so I went to their homes to share communion. They opened their hearts to me and enjoyed correcting my broken English.[21]

I was their pastor, and they were like parents to me. One even introduced me to her beautiful daughter, which triggered no little gossip. But I was still not ready to start a family, and unbeknownst to me, God was preparing the perfect wife for me back in the Middle East.

I returned to Gaza again in 1996. This time, my brother Salem was dying.

---

[21] My precious "landlady," Anita Brandow, would check my sermons on Saturday nights and help me with some of the words or pronunciations.

Life had been very difficult for him. He used to have a small photography studio, and one day, Israeli soldiers came to our house and took my brother away. He was very afraid. They said he had taken a picture of somebody wanted by Israel who had used it to make a false ID. They put a bag over Salem's head and interrogated him for a day. But my brother was innocent, and they finally returned him to us.

In 1994, the gas tank in our kitchen exploded. Salem was badly burned, and it affected him mentally, emotionally and physically for the rest of his life.

Salem and our sisters died one after the other, but our church had no place to bury them. We had to go to the Greek Orthodox church to bury them in their cemetery. Each tribe has a designated amount of land to bury their dead; the Massads have twelve square yards.

In September, 1999, my good friend Dr. David Johnston, at Fuller, suggested that I start a ministry to reach out to people in Gaza and to help them with their physical and spiritual needs. We called it Christian Mission to Gaza (CM2G) and registered it in California
as a non-profit organization with tax exempt status under IRC 501(c)(3).

I returned home the following month, fulfilling my promise to my father, and resumed pastoring at Gaza Baptist Church, which had been without a shepherd for
eight years. At the same time, I began relief work among the needy—both Christians and Muslims—under the auspices of the new CM2G ministry. I also joined the teaching staff at Bethlehem Bible College.

Then, the Second Intifada exploded.

I could no longer go to Bethlehem. So I taught theology to students and leadership to PA leaders through the BBC extension and Bible Society in Gaza

4. Girl from Kuwait

I MET SUHAD December 16, 1999 in an Internet chat room.

The Middle East is tribal and the Christian community is relatively small, so we immediately knew a little about one another by our last names. Also, one of my friends knew one of Suhad's cousins and her family's reputation. So it didn't take long before things began to develop.

Because she was from a Catholic background, Suhad didn't know what a pastor was. The only church leaders she was familiar with were priests, so she had to look it up.

Suhad's parents are from Beit Sahour, a tiny town adjacent to Bethlehem in the West Bank. But because Jordan ruled the West Bank from 1948 to 1967, she and her family were actually Jordanian citizens.

Suhad was born in Kuwait in 1970. When she was in her early twenties, her mother was diagnosed with acute Leukemia and died ten days later. Suhad was devastated. Eventually, her father remarried.

An excellent student, Suhad was in the top ten percent of students in Kuwait. Then, the First Gulf War began and, because of harassment and intimidation by Iraqi security forces, Suhad's family was forced, along with 200,000 other Palestinians, to flee. They settled in Jordan, where Suhad continued her education at the University of Jordan, went on to earn a master's degree in biology and began teaching.

The year 2000 was a whirlwind for me. I met Suhad's parents in March, we were engaged in May, I finished my Ph.D. in June and we were married in September. I had waited a long time to get married, and when I met the right girl, I wasted no time.

Actually, I was amazed that she accepted my proposal because of all the fear attached to my family's disease. I told her about it, of course, and as a biologist, she understood exactly what it meant. Once, I asked her why the disease did not discourage her from marrying me.

"First of all, because you told me in advance. That helped me to trust you. Second, the way you love your family and help them made a big difference."

Her parents were more of a challenge. Her father didn't understand what it meant to be Protestant, much less Evangelical. The first evening, he and Suhad's stepmother began to question me. They thought I was a Jehovah's Witness or something like that. They wanted to know who I was, what I did and what marriage meant to me personally and within my denomination. I tried to be patient, but I felt like a man under interrogation.

When I knew I wanted to get married, I asked one of my sisters for a blood sample and sent it to Cyprus to find out which kind of Muscular Dystrophy she had. As I said, my family was in denial and, until then, I had never heard of Myotonic MD. Suhad's father wanted to wait until we got the test results, but she insisted, and when he realized she was determined, he agreed.

After the results came back, I had myself tested and praised God when I learned that one more member of our family had escaped the debilitating disease.

One of the things that touched my heart deeply about Suhad was that, when we were engaged, she visited Gaza and, when she saw my sisters, she hugged them. She truly loved and served them.

The wedding presented another small challenge. Catholics like to drink, which was difficult for me as a Baptist. But we eventually figured out a way to have a wedding without alcohol.

Before his death, my father had begun to build a second floor on our house, and I completed the work with the money I had saved from pastoring First Baptist Church of Azuza.

Things were difficult at first, as it often is with newlyweds. Sometimes I didn't have even fifty cents in my pocket. We had no kitchen for several weeks and no car. But God was always faithful,[22] and Suhad never complained. She was able to get an early withdrawal of her Social Security money from Jordan which helped us buy a refrigerator and other things.

We worked together a lot. Suhad became Director of The Teacher's Bookstore, the public name of the Gaza branch of The Bible Society, and she led our AWANA program.[23]

We translated four of John Maxwell's powerful leadership training books into Arabic and were permitted to use them to teach leadership courses to church leaders and to hundreds of Muslims who worked for the PA. Upon completion, we gave them Bibles, because Scripture is the source of all John Maxwell's leadership principles. One Muslim doctor came to us in tears.

"How can I reconcile what you are teaching with the corruption in the PA?"

She realized that, without morals and ethics, Palestinians will never be able to rule themselves and develop into a strong, righteous, independent country.

Every week in our church, we ministered to about 200 people, some of whom were Muslims. Once, healing evangelist Peter Youngren came to Gaza, and we had a healing service at the beach. About half of the people who came for prayer and healing were Muslims. We also had an impact on some Israelis.

---

[22] When I was editing the manuscript of this book, I noticed that I repeated a lot that God is faithful. I understand that it's not necessarily good writing, but it's right theology, so I decided to leave it in.

[23] AWANA (Approved Workmen Are Not Ashamed, 2 Timothy 2:15) is a global organization established in Illinois in 1950 that provides "Bible-based evangelism and discipleship solutions for ages 2-18."

There was a Jewish military post near our church. From there, a Messianic IDF soldier could hear our services, and said he wished he could come and worship with us. He had been trained not to look a Palestinian in the eye.

"One day," he said, "a Palestinian man approached me and the Lord told me to look him in the eye. I did, and I realized he was a fellow believer and we had seen one another somewhere before. I didn't care about the training. Even with my weapons on, I went over and hugged him."

The person of Jesus Christ can bring us together when politics and everything else fails.

Baptisms were cause for great celebration in Gaza as well as in heaven, and much of the credit goes to Magdy and Rima Anwar, who served with us between 1999 and 2004. Magdy was raised in a Coptic home in Egypt. Rima was Jordanian. But their hearts knew no borders. The Lord sent Magdy to us after he had served as a pastor in Jerusalem for two years.

"I was so happy about this opportunity," he said, "because in Gaza there are only a few Christians! I would
be swimming in an ocean of Muslims!"

They dove right in.

Their home was open 24/7. Their table offered fruits and nuts and other delicious things to eat and drink, but the singles who thought of the Anwar's home as their second home did not come just for the food. They came for the unconditional love, acceptance and friendship Magdy and Rima offered. Many came to Christ through their ministry and were baptized, which had never happened before in this church.

His four years with us, Magdy said, "was the best opportunity we ever had to see people becoming believers in Jesus and to be able to disciple so many people."

I have never been in prison, but Gaza is what some describe as "the world's largest open-air prison." As Palestinians, everything in our lives is controlled by the Israelis or dependent upon outsiders. As Palestinian *Christians*, it is even worse. We live in the midst of fires—the fires of militant Muslims, traditional churches and the fire of occupation. Our challenge is to love and to live our faith day after day in the midst of these fires.

Fire burns, but it also refines. My faith was refined more in the fires of the Middle East than in the previous decade of Bible study in America.

Greek Orthodox priests telephoned me once and said they wanted to see me. When I arrived, the room was filled with church trustees and a priest.

"We have heard that people are coming to you to be baptized," they said. "Don't baptize them!"

When I said respectfully that I could not do as they asked, one of the trustees turned to the priest and said,
"Do whatever you have to."

"That's not fair," said another. "He is a Baptist. This is what he believes, and you cannot control it."

But the others agreed with the first trustee.

Afterward, they distributed a letter throughout the community, charging me with consorting with the devil and trying to drive people away from the Greek Orthodox Church. They even gave fliers to the children in our AWANA club, telling them to stay away. But the children loved AWANA too much and continued to come. Some even tore the leaflets on the spot.

After the threats, an elderly Greek Orthodox man visited us one Sunday evening and heard us praying for his priests. He was shocked.

"I have heard what the priests say about you," he said, "and here you are praying for them."

God answers all sorts of prayers, but He seems particularly fond of impossible ones. For me, one of those impossible prayers was becoming an American citizen.

One day, the mail contained an official-looking envelope from the USCIS. It contained Form N-445, my Notice of Naturalization Oath Ceremony. When I arrived for my interview, the immigration officer asked me where I was born, and I said Gaza, Palestine. But "Palestine" did not appear on his list of countries. So he put "Israel."

It is hard to explain, but this hurt me deeply, even when I was so excited about my answered prayer. I explained that I was not born in Israel. He knew I was not Jewish, and he was very understanding and sympathetic, but he said he had to put down the name of a country that was officially recognized by Washington.

"No matter," he said kindly, "tomorrow you are going to become a US citizen."

The next day, I checked in and surrendered my Permanent Resident (Green) Card.

The hall throbbed with hundreds of men and women from every country in the world, it seemed, dressed in their best as befitting such a solemn and meaningful event.

We pledged:

> *"I hereby declare, on oath, that I absolutely and
> entirely renounce and abjure all allegiance and
> fidelity to any foreign prince, potentate, state, or
> sovereignty, of whom, or which I have heretofore been
> a subject or citizen; that I will support and defend the
> Constitution and laws of the United States of America
> against all enemies, foreign and domestic . . ."*

My hand trembled when they handed me my Certificate of Naturalization. It is and will always remain a great privilege for me and my wife and daughters to be citizens of the greatest country in the world.

Sadly, even as a US citizen with an American passport, I am still treated as a Palestinian at the border crossings and checkpoints because I must carry a Palestinian ID. Such is the unjust and paradoxical life of a Palestinian.

Before the end of the Second Intifada, Suhad went to Amman to visit her family. She had a Jordanian passport, but Israel had given her only a single-entry visa
and would not allow her to come back to Gaza. When she went to the Israeli Embassy to appeal, they stamped "Rejected" on her passport, which meant she could not even reapply for six months.

We asked the brethren to pray.

Nothing happened for four to five months. Then, a Christian lawyer in Jerusalem carried our case to the Israeli Supreme Court.

Suhad recalls that, "it was not an easy period. I was frustrated and felt that life was unfair. I did nothing wrong to lose my right to be back with my husband in our home.

"Each day, the hope to return home decreased. Taking the case to the Supreme Court made me feel even more frustrated that we were stuck in a big problem, and my frustration put more pressure on Hanna, traveling back and forth between Gaza and Jordan. With all of his responsibilities for the church and his family, it was not easy. At the same time, however, knowing that many people around the world were praying for our situation made me realize that I belong to a bigger family than I could ever imagine.

"I tried to use my time in Jordan in many different ways. One of the things I like is cross-stitching, so I did different wall hangings, which I took later to my home in Gaza. And I did a tablecloth for Gaza Baptist Church. Every time I see it now, it reminds me of the hard time we passed through and how God's hands were always there to take us from one stage to another.

"Being there at that time also gave me an opportunity to help a young man from our church arrange for his marriage to a young lady from the West Bank. Because of the restrictions, the two families were forced to meet in Jordan."

Several months later, the court ruled that Suhad could come home to us. Once again, however, she was given only a single-entry visa, but we were very happy.

Despite the fact that Suhad was married to an American citizen and finally was granted an American passport,[24] when she went to Jordan in June 2006 to deliver our second daughter, Jolene, she again was not permitted to return. I was unable to leave Gaza due to travel restrictions, so I saw Jolene for the first time two weeks after her birth.

The last week of November, 2006, Suhad received a telephone call and was told it was from the office of the prime minister.

"Which one," she wondered. "Jordan, Palestine or Israel?"

It was an Israeli official we had never met. We assume that someone who had received our newsletter had contacted him.

"Go to the Israeli Embassy tomorrow," he told Suhad.

"I just went yesterday," she explained, "and they rejected me again."

"Don't worry," he assured her. "Just go."

When she arrived, everything had changed.

"Oh, here you are!" the embassy guard said happily. "We've been waiting for you."

And they sat down with her and were very kind and helpful. They didn't even charge her the fee for the visa.

The young man who had made this possible was one of the kindest human beings we ever met. He continued to help us for the next year. Then, he simply seemed to disappear, like the angels people sometimes encounter without realizing it.[25]

---

[24] Though Suhad became a US citizen when we married, she had to meet additional qualifications in order to obtain an American passport. Normally, people who live overseas must live in the US for three years. But because she and I are officially missionaries to a church, the government counts our time overseas. So she had to live in America for only one year, which she did during our sabbatical in 2008.

[25] Hebrews 13:2.

Family separations continue to be a hardship for Palestinians to this day. Some have not seen family members for many years due to draconian travel restrictions.

Prior to 9/11, most Muslims were secular and cultural but not fanatical. After the attack on America, all that changed. But the ones who wanted to hurt us were still a very small group in comparison. Most of the people in Gaza didn't belong to Hamas or Fatah or any other militant group. They just wanted to live and to raise their children and have a future. I, too, neither accept nor condone the purpose or behavior of Hamas.

After the Coalition went into Iraq, things became even more difficult, especially for Christians who are connected in the minds of Islamic militants with what they perceive as a "Christian" America.

Christian Zionists,[26] particularly Baptists, cause additional problems for Christians in the Middle East when they are very vocal and expressive in their unconditional support for Israel. And the sign on our church reads Gaza *Baptist* Church.

Unfortunately, many evangelical Christians have built a theology around the Abrahamic covenant.

I will bless those who bless you, and whoever curses you I will curse; and all peoples on earth will be blessed through you.[27]

Christian Zionists do not even believe we exist. I was speaking at a church in Minnesota once, and between the two services a man came up to talk to me.

---

[26] I use the term Zionist to describe support of the movement to re-establish a Jewish homeland within the geographical borders of Israel marked out in biblical verses including Genesis 15:18, 17:8 and Exodus 23:31. To accomplish this, however, Israel would have to occupy not only the West Bank and Gaza but also Jordan and Cyprus and pieces of Egypt, Iraq, Syria, Lebanon, and parts of Kuwait, Saudi Arabia and Turkey.

[27] Genesis 12:3.

"How can you call yourself a Palestinian?" he said, rudely. "There is no such thing."

"Get over it," some visiting Christians have actually said to us over the years. "God gave your land to Israel."

So I ask them, "You mean I have to lose the home I inherited from my parents and grandparents because my heavenly Father needs to fulfill a prophecy?"

I do not see this in the Bible. But the Bible does speak extensively against injustice. Amos 5:24 declares, "let justice roll on like a river, righteousness like a never-failing stream!" And Micah 6:8 teaches, "what does the Lord require of you? To act justly and to love mercy and to walk humbly with your God."

Christian Zionists confuse today's State of Israel with biblical Israel, the former being mostly a secular entity that, rejecting Jesus, rejects the God of Abraham.

"I am the way and the truth and the life. No one comes to the Father except through me."[28]

The Apostle Paul distinguished between the two Israel's: God's Israel and the Israel that rejected God.

For not all who are descended from Israel are Israel. Nor because they are his descendants are they all Abraham's children. On the contrary, 'It is through Isaac that your offspring will be reckoned.' In other words, it is not the children by physical descent who are God's children, but it is the children of the promise who are regarded

as Abraham's offspring.[29]

---

[28] John 14:6.
[29] Romans 9:6-8.

And again.

> *A person is not a Jew who is one only outwardly, nor*
> *is circumcision merely outward and physical. No, a*
> *person is a Jew who is one inwardly; and*
> *circumcision is circumcision of the heart, by the*
> *Spirit, not by the written code.*[30]

Scripture, however, makes it very clear that God is not finished with Israel.

> *I do not want you to be ignorant of this mystery,*
> *brothers and sisters, so that you may not be conceited:*
> *Israel has experienced a hardening in part until the*
> *full number of the Gentiles has come in, and in this*
> *way all Israel will be saved. As it is written: "The*
> *deliverer will come from Zion; he will turn*
> *godlessness away from Jacob. And this is my covenant*
> *with them when I take away their sins."*[31]

God came to Israel once before, and He is coming to them now. There are thousands of Messianic Jews in Israel and around the world. And He will complete His work among the Jewish people in the future.

We can trust God to fulfill His own prophecies without much help from us. Our responsibility is to speak to as many people as we can about our Savior and against injustice in a loving way.

---

[30] Romans 2:28-29.
[31] Romans 11:25-27.

5. Suhad's Perspective

PEOPLE FROM MANY COUNTRIES used to live in Kuwait. In the Middle East, children inherit the citizenship of their father, regardless of where they are born. So, though I was born in Kuwait, I was Jordanian, like my father. Non-Kuwaitis were not allowed to buy homes, so we all used to rent apartments.

My family lived for eighteen years in the apartment where I was born, and our neighbors were like a big family, always being there for each other, celebrating with each other and helping each other in any situation.

Kuwait is a Muslim country, and the schools in the Middle East are totally different than in America, regarding the teaching of religion. In public schools, or even Christian private schools, teaching about Christianity is not allowed. Only Islam is taught, and as a member of the Christian minority, I was sometimes the only one in a class of thirty-five. I had to stay in the class, hearing their teaching, sometimes including criticism against Christianity, while working on other subjects. So, the only way to learn about the Bible was through Sunday schools, church youth groups and my parents, especially my mom who encouraged us to be there. Friday was a weekend day, so we used to go to church on Friday because everyone works or goes to school on Sunday.

I was an A-student, with a GPA of 96.1 percent and was ranked 155 of all high schoolers in Kuwait in 1988. My parents expected a lot from me, since I have a very intelligent older sister.

Math was my favorite subject. In second grade, my math teacher let me help her correct classwork. In fourth grade, I helped with the quizzes. There were no computers or printers, so I made carbon copies for thirty students, graded them and gave the results to my teacher.

In 9th grade, I came home once crying, and my parents and grandparents thought there was some disaster. I showed them my report card. In math, I had only gotten 99.5 instead of 100 percent! Of course, my grandparents told everybody when they headed home.

I can't forget when I was in the 4th grade and the head of Islamic studies asked me to come to her office. Some of my Muslim friends were also there.

"You are really exceptional," she said. "Everything in you is just wonderful. An A-student, polite, organized, responsible, honest, caring, helping others, etc. The only thing you are not is Muslim, so why not to be converted to Islam? We want to convince you to do that."

I was in shock. So my first response was, "Why don't you become a Christian? I have all of these good traits because I am a Christian."

I told her I believe in my Bible. At that time, I did not read the Bible, but being raised in a Catholic family where my mom was committed to the church, one didn't even think about converting.

"But your Bible is corrupted," she said. "It is not the original one."

I kept calm and listened, but inside I was boiling. When she finally stopped talking, I told her, "Sorry, but I am not convinced at all with what you said."

I went home feeling frustrated but did not mention anything to my parents. I was not an outgoing child. I kept it all inside me. But the next day, I took the copy of the New Testament that we had at home to school. I went back to the teacher in front of some of my Muslim friends, took out my New Testament and asked her to
please show me which verses had been changed. Where are they? What are the original verses?

She was in shock and said, "I do not know. *They* say so," without mentioning who she was referring to. I was delighted inside that she was not able to answer.

"Okay, then you did not convince me, so please do not ask me this question again. But maybe there will be time to convince you about the truth."

That was the last time she talked about that topic.

I think being a member of a minority and feeling the pressure from the community played a role inside my heart to know and learn more. I was blessed to be raised in a Christian family. Being in a Catholic church, we learned a lot about Jesus' life, miracles, His death and resurrection and about church traditions.

I was an active, and the youngest, member in the Catholic church youth group in Kuwait. We had a Coptic leader with his wife, probably the age of my parents. They used to bring cassette tapes from Egypt with Christian songs. Such a thing was not allowed to be sold in Kuwait, and one of my responsibilities was to listen to these songs and write out the lyrics, so we could use them to teach the Sunday school kids how to sing them.

My mother's sudden death in 1992, at age 47, was a big event to me. She was in a big hospital room with other cancer patients. She showed sympathy for them without knowing she had been attacked as well.

I did medical lab training there and knew the nurses and staff, knew about her condition of acute leukemia and asked the staff not to share anything with her. I went to visit with her every day, trying to pretend that I was strong and joking around with her, but as soon as I left the room I could not stop crying.

Although she underwent chemotherapy treatments a couple of times, she did not experience any hair loss or any other side effects. She asked me about it once, and I tried to change the topic by telling her that her medicine is affected by light, which is why they covered it with silver wrapping.

Again and again, I went to the library and searched my books, since I am a biologist, trying to learn more about acute leukemia, and everything I read called it a "short-term disease." I thought that meant she would be healed in a short time. But her doctor explained that it meant I could lose her at any time.

One day, she called home before I left for the university. She wanted me to get her some hair shampoo and help her wash her hair because she had an IV in her hand. I was shocked to see that my mom was not even able to wash her hair by herself.

I went to the hospital after I finished at the university and brought what she had requested, hoping inside that she would not ask me to help her because I did not want to see her that weak. Fortunately, the nurse, earlier that day, had helped her wash her hair. After her death, I wished I had those days back, wished to hug her and wash her hair.

When my final exam approached, she asked me not to come to the hospital so I could study. So I went over after the exam and talked with her in the ICU. I couldn't believe that her eyes were covered and she was hooked up to a bunch of machines.

"If I were in your shoes," the doctor told me, "I would remove all the instruments and let her pass away."

"You do not know," I said, crying and shouting, "she is my mom!"

My mother was a young, sweet lady, full of energy, a caring person who gained respect from all who met her.
She was a godly woman, committed to church, a praying mother, singing Christian songs at home, taking good care of her family and extended family, a mom who was waiting for her kids to graduate from college and get married, anxious to see her grandkids.

So, she passed away without knowing or feeling what was attacking her. To the end, she kept looking healthy, bright and full of energy. And the only thing she was able to see was the graduation of my older sister two months before the Iraqi invasion. That made me mad.

Why did that happen? What was her fault? What were our faults to lose our mom at that young age? I was really angry and upset with God. She was a godly woman, so why did He not interfere? Why did He allow her to pass through this? Why did He allow us to suffer after her death? Many questions with no answers. I was really looking forward to the day when I would wake up and discover that it was all a bad dream. But that day never came.

I should have graduated before Mom's death, but because of the Gulf War and transfer to another university, I lost about half of my credentials. That made me mad, too.

It took me years to reconcile with God.

I met Hanna on the Internet, and we started to chat and discuss some of my unanswered questions. I felt I could ask him freely because he was a pastor. I was shocked by some of his answers and the proofs he gave me from the Bible. I also learned that things I thought were in the Bible were just religious traditions. I never thought that God wanted a personal relationship with us. I though He was just up there, watching us, in control.

The process of growth was a long one for me. It was not a single step or event, maybe because I analyze everything. I needed proof for everything. But faith is believing things you can't see or prove.

I continued to grow in my faith and experience a personal relationship with God, especially after Hanna and I got married and I moved to Gaza. Seeing little kids in Sunday School, memorizing verses, knowing all the Bible stories, singing with joy, praying to the Lord impressed me. I joined Bible study groups in Gaza with Rima Anwar, who took care of me as if she was my mom. I started to look for more resources to learn from. I took online Bible study lessons, started searching the books, explanations of the Bible verses that I used to read or memorize without knowing the exact meaning.

My dad used to go to church just occasionally. He was a hard worker, determined, honest, enthusiastic, a social person who showed his caring and passion by his actions. He had a great sense of humor and stayed strong as he faced the challenges he encountered in his life.

But my dad had a problem with the tradition of confessing sins to a priest, which he never did except when he got married. He did not believe this was the right way to get forgiveness. Joking around, he told the priest to just consider that he committed every sin once. The priest was shocked and asked my father if he ever killed anybody.

"No," my father replied.

So the priest started to ask him about other sins, and my father said "no."

At the end, my dad asked the priest to consider all the sins, other than those, as yes.

Hearing this from my dad at a young age lead me to think, why do I need to confess my sins to the priest for forgiveness? I can just go directly to God and ask Him.

I am one of seven, in the middle of two brothers and two sisters, with two younger step-brothers from my father's marriage after my mother died. My father's remarriage was as much of a challenge for me as it was for my stepmother. He felt that the family had been hit by a rocket by my mother's death and had started to scatter, and he wanted to gather us all together again.

For me, it was not easy to see another woman replace my mother. It took me a long time to accept the reality and have inner peace. It was hard for my step-mom as well, finding herself suddenly responsible for a big family, needing to understand our needs, accepting our griefs and sadness and getting used to our way of living. But after those years, I am so thankful for my dad and my step-mom who have been there for me, even in the midst of my challenges and struggles.

I remember when my sister and I visited our brother Eyad in Greece, just before the Iraqi invasion of Kuwait. He gave us a tour of the area, and we had dinner at a restaurant. After dinner, we asked for coffee, and they brought us something similar to Turkish coffee—heavy and served in small cups.

After we finished our coffee, Eyad shook the remainder of the grounds, flipped them upside down on a plate waited a couple of minutes for the grounds to dry.
He began to point out maps and shapes and diagrams in the dregs. Then, he looked at them, pretending that he could explain what each shape meant and what might happen in the future. Suddenly, people started bringing their coffee cups to Eyad, asking him to read their fortunes. My sister and I started to laugh and asked him to stop. It seemed that many people there believed in such a thing, just as in Middle Eastern countries, so we had to wait hours until he finished. Some of them knew
it was just for fun.

My sister Daed is my best friend. We're just two years apart. We played together all the time and never fought. I always admire her for her organization, achievements, hard work and caring. I learned a lot from being close to her. Daed, too, is an A-student. Her high school GPA was 98.3. She ranked 27th out of all the high schoolers in Kuwait in 1986. Daed wanted to study medicine, but that was impossible at Kuwait University because she didn't rank first or second. So she was accepted in engineering.

At that time, a local organization called my dad and told him they would give her a scholarship to study whatever she likes in America because she ranked in the top fifty. They used to do that every year. My father thanked them but refused their offer, concerned about how she would live on her own in the US at that time. So Daed studied civil engineering at Kuwait University and finished early. Fortunately, she graduated just two months before the invasion, so she didn't have to transfer to another university and study for two more years like I did.

Another brother, Saed, loves soccer. He can tell you all the teams playing, who is playing whom, scores, etc. When he was a toddler, he used to ask for the sports page, even before he was able to pronounce the words correctly, to look at pictures of players and the games. When he was eight, we had a vacation in Spain where some of my uncles live. They got Saed a football, and he was so excited about it. One day, we went to the park, which we didn't have in Kuwait. We were happy just to walk, run and eat ice cream, and of course Saed was enjoying his time with his ball. Suddenly, we found him running with his ball in a big circle, with a dog running close behind, and he wouldn't stop until someone caught the dog. We don't have pets in the Middle East. We still talk and laugh about that day.

My sister Nahed entered first grade when I was in the eleventh. Her nickname is Nana, and she didn't learn her real name until she started school where nicknames are not allowed. Nahed was petite, so my mom did not stop giving her a milk bottle and pacifier until she started to go to school. One day, she asked the teacher to use the bathroom. Instead, she came to my class, crying and asking me for her bottle and pacifier. Poor sis.

My brother Shahd was our baby toy at home. When he was born, we were old enough to enjoy him, so we didn't allow him to cry. Many hands would compete to hold him, which challenged his mom. When he graduated from kindergarten, the school had a ceremony and the children put on a little performance. Shahd played the king. Unfortunately, he had a fever that day, so he had taken some medicine. During the play, he urgently needed to use the restroom. So, the principal paused the play and announced that the King had to go to the bathroom and everyone would just have to wait until he came back. She could not hide her smile.

Majd is my youngest brother, who I used to take, with Shahd, to restaurants and places of entertainment. He was two years old when Hanna started visiting, before we got engaged. Whenever he saw Hanna sitting beside me, Majd would squeeze between us. During our wedding dance, I felt something pulling my wedding dress. I looked down, and there was Majd, tugging at it, just letting me know he was there.

When Iraq invaded Kuwait on August 2, 1990 and all communication with the country was shut down, our family lost connection with one another. My mother and Nahed were in Palestine for summer vacation. Daed and I could not join them because it was difficult to get a visiting permit from Israel, so, we went to Greece to visit Eyad who was studying there. My father and Saed remained in Kuwait.

Eventually, we got a message from my father, telling us not to return to Kuwait but to go to Jordan and stay with our aunt. Surprisingly, my mom had gotten permission from Israel to be with her and had received a permit. So my sister Daed and I went to Beit Sahour, under Israeli occupation at that time, for about two months until we got a message from my father to come back.

When we returned, Kuwait was a different and strange country. It used to be clean, but it was no longer. We had to wait in lines in front of the bakery to get a pack of pita bread and do the same thing at other stores in order to buy supplies. Every morning, we had to check our cars to see if they were still standing on wheels or blocks of stone. We had to park our cars so the fuel doors faced each other, so no one could open them and steal our gas. Everywhere we drove, Iraqi checkpoints searched cars for weapons. And soldiers often asked us for food.

When I went to Kuwait University to get my official papers, I collected my papers from the floor. Desks were gone. Computer monitors had been stolen out of their cases, the thieves thinking that they were TV sets.

It was intolerable for me, having been born and raised in Kuwait, to see it that way. We had considered it our country. Now, everything was gone. Nothing would ever be the same again. I could not even imagine a future there. Most of our friends and their families had left Kuwait, though some did not because no country would accept them.

My father was very concerned about our safety. He wanted all of us to leave Kuwait without risking any of us. He had lived in Kuwait since 1960 and married my mother five years later. You can imagine the stuff we had after a quarter of a century. And now it was time to leave.

Many families who lived in Kuwait had gone back to their home countries—Egypt, Syria, Lebanon. But for us and many others, it was totally different. We are Palestinians who did not have official documents to be identified as Palestinians. Instead, we had Jordanian passports, because the West Bank was considered to belong to Jordan. And so, Jordan became our destination.

Even so, our situation was amazingly better than Palestinians from Gaza. They carried Egyptian travel documents, not passports. They had nowhere to travel, because no country would accept them, although some were able to go to Yemen.

We packed everything in boxes, with glassware wrapped piece by piece. My mom loved having kitchen tools, utensils, etc., so she kept a lot of it, and it had to be packed carefully. Suitcases filled with clothing, boxes of kitchen stuff, furniture, computer, books, blankets, carpets . . . all had to fit in one truck. Twenty-five years packed and headed for an unknown destination.

We had finished loading the truck, exhausted from the packing process and with mixed feelings about what was going on, when two Iraqi soldiers came to our apartment. We were scared. What are they looking for?

To our shock, they told us, "You are traveling now. We hope you will have a safe journey. But if you have any food left over, please give it to us. If you have any tea, sugar, rice, flour, bread, canned food . . . anything that you are not taking with you." My father gave them all the remaining groceries.

He, one of my sisters and I had cars, so we loaded up and headed out.

It was a long trip from Kuwait (Region 19, an Iraqi Governate, after the invasion) to Baghdad, then on to Jordan in December 1990. We were six families, including uncles and cousins, traveling together in six cars, stuffed with kids, clothes, blankets and food. We all moved together. There were no cellphones then, so we constantly checked on one another through the car mirrors and communicated with hand and arm signs.

We stopped for a lot of bathroom breaks because of so many kids. So, when a middle-car kid needed to stop, the cars in front would continue to drive until noticing in the mirrors that the other cars were not there. Of course, there were no rest areas at all from Kuwait to Baghdad to the border. Not like in America.

After leaving Baghdad, we reached a bridge that had been closed. A policeman asked us to take another road, which would add a couple hours to our trip. Of course, we had no maps, no GPS. We were just following signs. My dad and uncles got out of the car and talked with the policeman about the reason for the closing. That's when we learned that the guy made his own toll, not allowing anyone to cross without paying. So we did, and he allowed us to cross.

When we reached the Iraq side of the Jordanian border, we were shocked to see hundreds and hundreds of cars waiting to be checked. It was mid-December in the desert, and the nights were cold.

The first night passed with no one being able to sleep because we were all sitting in the cars. To relieve the stress on everyone, my dad and uncles decided to put all the kids in one or two cars with their mothers and to cross the border without luggage. I stayed with my dad for two more nights on the border.

Finally, our turn came. In the middle of the night. A customs officer started checking our truck for prohibited items, which he said included our personal computer and university books. He said these were owned by the government and not allowed to leave the country. My dad was with him up in the truck and told him the computer and books belonged to us. If we pay him, the officer said, he would hide them so the supervisor would not see them.

What! Are we buying our personal computer and books again? But it was the only option for my dad if he wanted all our luggage to be released and to get through the jammed up, filthy border.

Several hours after we entered Jordan, we reached my aunt's house. She was shocked to see me looking yellowish. She started giving me a lot of water to drink, but it took several days before I felt normal again.

58

We began to clean the apartment we rented. It was small, like a box, jammed with our furniture and other possessions. I remember when I awoke the first morning, running out of the bedroom because it was like a storage room.

A month after we moved to Jordan, the Gulf War started. People there were scared. They started to tightly tape their windows shut, terrified of chemical weapons.

We didn't do any of that. We did not feel afraid. We felt things would not be worse than what we had already gone through.

The Internet was relatively new in Jordan. Out of curiosity one day, I logged into a chatroom. It was not a dating site, just people meeting people, making friends. It was new for Hanna as well, because he had just returned from the US.

When I met Hanna online, I was glad that I was talking to a pastor, which I thought was like a Catholic priest who does not marry. So chatting with him was interesting, because I felt I could talk without being misunderstood. When I told my family about Hanna and that I had met him online, it was a new experience for them. It wasn't even that common in our culture at that time.

When Hanna started to talk openly and honestly about his family, and I started to hear and feel how he cared about them, I felt peace. I felt this guy knows exactly what family means. He will take care of me.

I never thought I would be married to a Palestinian from Gaza, much less live in Gaza. I remember friends in Kuwait whose parents refused to let them marry Gazans because of all the troubles they had living and traveling. Also, neither I nor my family knew that there were any Christians in Gaza. But God had a bigger plan for me than I could ever dream of.

Moving from Kuwait to Jordan made it easier for me to settle in Gaza. It was still stressful though because of the warzone, and I couldn't stay in Gaza without renewing my visa. The process was long, and soon the visa would expire and I would have to apply again. Once we were married, Hanna applied for me to get a Palestinian ID, enabling me to stay as one married to a Gazan, but I never got it.

The pressures and uncertainties were eased by the warmth and simplicity of life in Gaza. And I was accepted both by Hanna's family and by the church family. After Joyce was born, however, we faced new challenges and disappointments. In Gaza, children have no rights, no assurance of security, no place safe to play—resources my brothers and sisters and I had in our childhood. I remember times when Joyce asked me for fruit yogurt and, because of the siege, we were unable to find any in the grocery stores.

Occasionally, I had to ask our American friends who visited Gaza from the West Bank or Jerusalem to bring a certain brand of diaper for her because of her very sensitive skin. Every time, I thanked God for our friends and bigger family, at the same time feeling sorry and sad that others had greater needs and couldn't fill them because they didn't have the global support we enjoyed.

But we still experienced sources of great joy.

Leading AWANA was a great experience for me, seeing the joy on the children's faces. The kids waited eagerly, week after week, to come to church. This is not to say that there weren't troublemakers. But the great thing about AWANA is that God is in it.

Khalil Sayegh was in one of the groups that caused trouble at that time. Many years later, we ran into him at Bethlehem Bible College while we were visiting.

"You don't know me," he said when we met. We didn't recognize him. Then, he introduced himself as the one who had been such a problem in AWANA.

"Even through that time," he said, "God was working on my heart and playing a role in my life. And much of what I am able to give today I learned in the AWANA club."

On the other hand, we had youngsters like Raghda, who was one of the very active kids in AWANA. She was a social, energetic, funny girl who loved to learn. Raghda grew up to become a delightful young lady, married one of the AWANA leaders, and they both became very active leading worship. We saw a lot of good fruit, and so many were impacted by the AWANA ministry.

As the rain and the snow come down from heaven, and do not return to it without watering the earth and making it bud and flourish, so that it yields seed for the sower and bread for the eater, so is my word that goes out from my mouth; It will not

return to me empty, but will accomplish what I desire and achieve the purpose for which I sent it.[32]

Sadly, AWANA ended after we left because most of the other leaders went to the West Bank with us.

Then, there was the Bible Society.

---

[32] Isaiah 55:10-11.

61

A lady from the Jabalia Refugee Camp had seven children, from newborn to eighteen years old. Her husband was mentally disabled. Five of her children suffered from physical and mental disabilities, and she came to us desperate, hopeless and afraid. For two years, we were able to walk alongside her and her family, pray with her, spend time with her, support her and meet her physical and spiritual needs.

One day, she told us she was pregnant and wanted to end the pregnancy, one way or another. We talked with her about God's love and gift and convinced her not to try to hurt the baby.

"You are the only one who stood with me," she said, "others pushed me out. Even my own people refused to help me."

She loved the Christian environment in the Bible Society to the point that her family members started to come to visit and spend time with us, and her son started to take English courses in our center.

We also taught women cross-stitch and gave them materials so they could support their families. Some would do Bible verses on wall hangings, and we used the opportunities to share with them about God's love. We continued to work with them until the day we had to close the Bible Society. Even after that, we kept receiving telephone calls from those ladies, crying and asking us to forgive what their people did against us. They told us they could no longer support their families since the Bible Society shut down, that nobody loves them and supports them the way we did.

As a young woman living in Gaza, I had simple dreams, like walking in the streets or at the beaches without being harassed because I didn't cover my hair, without having people stare at me as if I had done something wrong. I dreamt my family would be able to visit me and see where and how I live. But none of them could ever visit because of Gaza's travel restrictions. I had cousins, uncles and aunts in the West Bank, and I dreamed of spending Christmas or Easter with them. But again, because of travel restrictions, I was not able to travel 60 miles from Gaza to Beit Sahour.

6. Persecution

AS THE PERSECUTION ESCALATED, God's protection over us became palpable.

On May 17, 2004, during the Second Intifada, I picked up Suhad from the Bible Society. On the way home, I asked if she would mind if I stopped for gas. She said she was very tired and would rather just go home. She was pregnant, so we continued to the house. Less than five minutes later, we opened the door and started to enter when we heard a huge explosion. It sounded very close. Later, we learned that an Israeli helicopter gunship had fired a missile at a car, killing a 33-year-old Hamas leader named Imad Muhammad Ahmad Shabaneh. The car was hit at the intersection by the gas station where we would have been filling our gas tank.

December 10, 2004: Suhad gave birth to our first child. We named her Joyce.

"It was especially hard for me when Joyce was born," she recalls. "My family could not be with me at the hospital because of travel restrictions. Hanna's family could not be there because of their health restrictions. But when I went to the hospital, the hall and waiting room were filled with the people from our church family, praying for me and waiting to see their pastor's daughter. Even my doctor mentioned that he never saw so many people come before a surgery. And after she was born, a couple of my closest friends from church spent the night with me at the hospital, taking care of me and our baby."

Since I had become a US citizen the year before, Joyce was born an American citizen. But we still had to go to the American Embassy in Tel Aviv to prove it.

Unfortunately, Suhad was unable to leave Gaza because of her persistent visa problem. She couldn't even pass through the Erez Crossing into Israel. So, she stayed in the car on the Gaza side while I walked for twenty minutes along what seems like a big airport runway in the middle of nowhere with two-month-old Joyce in my arms. At the Israeli end, a representative from the US Embassy waited to see our daughter. He had come all the way down from Tel Aviv especially for this.

This was the first time Joyce had been separated from her mother, and she was crying out of control, even though I was her father. She had never cried like this before. For three hours, she never stopped screaming. I thought she was crying because she was hungry, and she was not weaned from the bottle.

Then, a Palestinian lady with a baby, also awaiting US personnel, offered to breastfeed Joyce. I gave her to the woman, and at first Joyce was ready to be fed. Then she realized that this was not her mother and she continued to scream. Suhad said when I brought her back that Joyce wouldn't take her eyes from her, and they seemed to accuse her of betraying her, which was very painful for Suhad.

The Israeli Occupation of Gaza ended in 2005. Eight thousand Israeli settlers from 21 settlements were relocated, and the soldiers returned to Israel. But though the Israelis were no longer there physically, they still controlled the land, sky and sea.

Before the persecution began, I felt it coming and talked about it with my congregation. Persecution is painful, I told them, but it should not be surprising.

Dear friends, do not be surprised at the fiery ordeal that has come on you to test you, as though something strange were happening to you. But rejoice inasmuch as you participate in the sufferings of Christ, so that you may be overjoyed when his glory is revealed.[33]

"You will be hated by everyone because of me," Jesus said, "but the one who stands firm to the end will be saved."[34]

"In fact," Paul taught Timothy, "everyone who wants to live a godly life in Christ Jesus will be persecuted."[35]

When was the last time you listened to a sermon entitled "The Gospel of Suffering?" The word *Gospel* comes from the Greek word *euaggelion*, which means good news. But there was never good news without a cross in the life of our Lord Jesus Christ. And if there was a cross in His life, we should not be surprised to encounter it in ours as well.

For it has been granted to you on behalf of Christ not only to believe in him, but also to suffer for him.[36]

We are able to see this life of pain and suffering and how to overcome it manifested in the public testimony of accepting Christ into our life, water Baptism and receipt of the Holy Spirit.

"I baptize you with water for repentance. But after me comes one who is more powerful than I, whose sandals I am not worthy to carry. He will baptize you with the Holy Spirit and fire."[37]

---

[33] 1 Peter 4:12-13.
[34] Matthew 10:22.
[35] 2 Timothy 3:12.
[36] Philippians 1:29.
[37] Matthew 3:11.

The *waters* of baptism separate us from the power of sin over our lives, as the Red Sea separated Israel from the power of Egypt.[38] Baptism's *flames*, however, refine and purify us.[39]

A common misunderstanding is the belief that, if I am suffering, God is punishing me.[40] This implies that Jesus failed in His mission to pay the full price for all the sins of all mankind, because some penalty remains for me to pay. Pain and suffering are the results of being a fallen people living in a fallen world. Some pain is the direct consequence of our choices. If I sit too long in the sun, I suffer a painful sunburn which might result in skin cancer. God did not give me sunburn or cancer as punishment for sitting too long in the sun. Sunburn is the result of natural law; cancer is a consequence of mankind's fall. But God can turn pain and suffering to our good.

> *And we know that in all things God works for the good of those who love him, who have been called according to his purpose.*[41]

> *For we do not have a high priest who is unable to empathize with our weaknesses, but we have one who has been tempted in every way, just as we are—yet he did not sin. Let us then approach God's throne of grace with confidence, so that we may receive mercy and find grace to help us in or time of need.*[42]

---

[38] 1 Corinthians 10:1-4.
[39] Isaiah 48:10; Daniel 12:10; 1 Peter 1:6-7.
[40] John 9:2.
[41] Romans 8:28.
[42] Hebrews 4:15-16.

"Keep on rejoicing," John Piper writes, "when you are thrown in the cellars of suffering, keep on rejoicing. When you dive in the sea of affliction, keep on rejoicing. In fact, keep on rejoicing, not in spite of the affliction but even because of it. This is not a little piece of advice about the power of positive thinking.

"This is a radical, supernatural way to respond to suffering. It is not in our power. It is not for the sake of honor. It is the way spiritual aliens and exiles live on the earth for the glory of the great King."[43]

In 2006, the persecution began in earnest.

Andrew van der Bijl is better known as Brother Andrew, the author of the Christian classic *God's Smuggler* and founder of Open Doors, a ministry that has served the persecuted Church worldwide since 1955.

Back in 1992, when Israel expelled 415 members of Hamas to a no-man's land in Southern Lebanon, Brother Andrew, compelled by Matthew 25, went to the men to check on their conditions and to visit their families. I think this is why Hamas sometimes tries to help us as evangelicals. A relationship developed, and he had the opportunity to share the Gospel with hundreds of Hamas members, including Hamas co-founder Dr. Mahmoud al-Zahar. The de facto leader of the government in Gaza, Zahar is sympathetic to Christians. He was nursed by a
Christian woman and grew up in a Christian community, a fact he likes to mention when he speaks to Christians. In 2003, an Israeli F-16 bombed his house in the Rimal neighborhood of Gaza, wounding him and his daughter Rima and killing his son Khaled and his bodyguard.

Brother Andrew took me to meet Zahar once. His philosophy is that, if we do not go to the Muslims with God's love, they will come to us with their bombs.

---

[43] Piper, John, "Why We Can Rejoice in Suffering," *Desiring God*, 23 October 1994.

Over the years, Gaza Baptist Church and CM2G have helped thousands of people, including Muslims, and I am sure these Muslims must ask themselves, "What makes these Christians love us and come to help us when the mosque is not helping us?"

Before Hamas came to power, we had much more freedom to go to the refugee camps with humanitarian relief. When we asked people if we could pray for them, most said yes, and we watched God answer many of those prayers. One day, I received a call from a leader of the Greek Orthodox Church in Gaza.

"Call this number," he said. "It is very important."

That was all he said, and he gave me a phone number.

"Are you Pastor Hanna?" a man's voice asked.

"Yes," I said.

"Come to my house, because I have something important to tell you."

I took along some of the young men from our church, and we went to the address he gave me. It belonged to Zahar.

"There is a group of twelve men," we were told, "who used to be part of Hamas but left to become more militant. These men were in the final preparations of putting forty kilograms of dynamite in your church building. Do you know somebody in the PA who can help you?"

"No," I said.

"It's okay now. Don't worry. We took care of it. We found them and were able to stop it."

Another time, we received a threatening letter with a Qur'anic verse that said, "We don't want you here, and if you stay, your life will be in danger." We stayed.

At 11:30 pm, February 3, my telephone rang at home. It was connected to the alarm system at the Bible Society. We were told there had been an attack. Two small pipe bombs had blown out the front door. Soon after, we received a note demanding that the bookstore close for good and threatening that the next attack would be bigger. So we repaired the door and closed for a month.

When nothing more happened, Suhad and the people at the Bible Society headquarters in Jerusalem agreed to reopen. The owner of the building, however, was very upset and tried to pressure Suhad to shut down for good because he was afraid for his property.

"Do you want to wait until somebody is murdered," he argued, "and then you'll want to close down?"

After we reopened, some of our team leaders began receiving threats.

Suhad was pregnant with our second child at the time and went to Amman to give birth. Jolene was born on July 19, 2006.

In December, Hamas tried to replace the PA police in Gaza, and a bloody battle broke out, with the Christian community caught in the crossfire. During the height of the coup, Palestinian Authority soldiers commandeered our six-story church building and fired down on Hamas from the roof.

As we evacuated the first floor library, the phone rang. A bullet struck Abu Ibrahim, our watchman, in the back, just as he reached out to answer it. He was critically wounded but survived.

Tragically, when our AWANA driver, a twenty-year-old newlywed, heard gunfire near his home and looked across the street to see what was going on, a sniper shot and killed him in front of his father.

Not infrequently, Suhad would have to grab the girls and get down on the floor at the sound of shooting. For years, Joyce was terrified even at the sound of fireworks.

Once, PA soldiers broke into the church and stole $4,000 worth of electrical equipment. Another time, we found a bullet where Suhad and I had been sitting in our garden the day before. We also frequently found ourselves caught in the crossfire between Hamas and Israel.

In 2006, before the Hamas coup in Gaza, we were driving home about 11 pm with our one-and-a-half-year-old daughter. As we neared the house, three Hamas gunmen stopped us, pointing guns into the car. Suddenly, one shouted to the others, "Stop! These are family."

God protected us, and we went home wondering what was happening in our neighborhood.

In the spring of 2007, an Israeli F-16 burst through the clouds and bombed a Hamas base about two hundred yards from our house, damaging our doors and nearly a dozen windows. Once again, God had protected us. Joyce was at a friend's house. Jolene was asleep in the master bedroom, and fortunately it was so hot out that Suhad had left the window over her head open a little, which minimized the damage and the concussive effect of the explosion. Suhad and I were in the living room, and I had my back to the window which had its drapes closed against the blazing sun.

How does a pastor preach to his congregation about God's provision and protection, love and mercy during military occupation, when fathers cannot earn enough money to provide for their families? When political factions shoot at one another in their neighborhoods? When attack helicopters and jet fighters thunder through the skies over their heads? When fishermen are not allowed to travel more than three nautical miles from shore, humanitarian aid is restricted, water is undrinkable and electrical power is unavailable?

One Sunday evening, the PA and Hamas were shooting at one another in the middle of the street during our service. I started to notice that the congregation was terrified. Some tried to hide under their seats. Bullets were coming close, almost hitting the church building. I had to stop preaching and send everyone home before things got much worse.

Another time, a shootout forced us to help fifty children escape through the back doors.

Sometimes, I would enter the church and find that the ceiling had collapsed. Other times, I could not enter at all because of the damage done by F-16s or Apache helicopters.

What do you do as a pastor? I prayed. We would comfort and encourage one another. I shared with our congregation from Psalm 91:

> *Whoever dwells in the shelter of the Most High will rest in the shadow of the Almighty. I will say of the Lord, "He is my refuge and my fortress, my God, in whom I trust."*

I cannot deny the circumstances, but I can declare the undeniable truth that God is our Provider, Refuge and Strength. I cannot deny that many of us are sick and infirm, but I can declare the undeniable truth that Jesus
took our sicknesses and diseases upon Himself and that His stripes made possible our healing.

We do better to look up and praise God for His undeniable character and acts and His immutable truth than to look at our circumstances and make excuses for Him. Nothing He has said or done requires an excuse. He is always God, always good, always right and just and perfect and loving and merciful and faithful. The problem is never with God. The problem has always been, and will continue to be, sin until He returns to rule a new heaven and a new earth. At the same time, we do what we can to help one another, whether Christian, Muslim or Jew.

The second attack at the Bible Society came on April 15, 2007.

At 2:30 am, the phone rang. I was told there had been a big explosion at the bookstore. I picked up Rami Ayyad and a few others from the church, and we drove through the empty streets.

I felt sick in my stomach as I stood in front of the store and saw the damage. As I shared my heart with the Lord, he said, "As I was with you with the first explosion, I am with you now. Fear not."

"Hanna, with other team members, went to the site directly after the explosion," Suhad recalls. "I could not go with them because the girls were too young to be left at the time. But I was in contact by phone with Hanna while he was there. It was not easy to feel that your people are working to destroy the good thing you are trying to do.

"The next morning, I told Hanna that I needed to go to the site because I was director of the Gaza branch of the Bible Society. He said that we can go together, but I insisted to go by myself.

"I was not sure what to expect to see, but my concern at that time was that, if anything more happens while I am at the site, Hanna will be available for our daughters. Of course, in the bookstore, I was not alone. Other team members were there. We started repairing the damage and did not close the Bible Society, which made the ones who caused the explosion even more aggressive."

After this explosion, many people—mostly Muslims—gathered to show support and solidarity. People knew that many good things had happened to their families through this ministry, and they were angry about what had happened.

Not long after the bombing, a young militant man came to the bookstore.

"Why don't you become a Muslim?" he asked Rami.

"Why don't you become a Christian?" Rami responded with a grin.

But the man was in no mood to be playful.

"We know how to make you one," he threatened.

In June, a Christian professor who taught at Palestine University in Gaza City was kidnapped and forced to convert to Islam, reportedly assisted by the president of the university.[44]

On Sunday, September 30, I preached a sermon asking, "How serious are we about our faith? Are we willing to lay down our lives?"

I felt it was in the spirit of prophecy.

---

[44] *Fact Sheets: Christians in the Palestinian Authority* (Updated May 2008), Jewish Virtual Library, a project of the American-Israeli Cooperative Enterprise (AICE), est. 1993.

7. Martyrdom

LATE THE FOLLOWING SATURDAY afternoon, October 6, we were all waiting for Rami to show up after work for a meeting of AWANA leaders. It was Ramadan, and we had the feeling something serious might have happened.

The previous Thursday, after work, Rami's taxi driver noticed three young men in a car behind them. They followed him all the way to his home. The next day, while he and his mother were eating, the telephone rang.

"What do you want?" Rami asked the caller, obviously upset. "Why are you calling me?"

Later, Suhad told him not to feel that he had to come to work. But Rami insisted.

At two o'clock, he wanted to listen to a popular praise song:

Lord, your love is sweeter than honey.
I am fully satisfied by my God.
The water of the world is bitter.
It cannot quench my thirst.
The world has nothing to offer
that can fill me like the love of Jesus.
You purchased me with your blood.
You made me like a king.
I scorn the sweet things of the world,
its honors, its pleasures and its gold.
If you think I will kneel before you,
you are wrong.
Whatever happens, my heart will be
fulfilled in the day I bow down in front of my
Sweetest One.[45]

---

[45] Loosely paraphrased from the Arabic.

He closed the bookstore at four, as usual. While we waited for him that Saturday, we were confident that no matter what, his faith would continue to be strong.

One of our team members finally reached Rami by phone.

"I am with some young men here," he said, "and it will be a long time before I will be able to come back."

We didn't know what to do or where to go. Since Hamas had taken over the government, no one knew what to expect or who was in charge of anything. So, we prayed, while his brothers went out and searched for him.

It was difficult trying to prepare my sermon that night. At 3 am, I tried to go to bed and called his cellphone again, but it had shut down at 6:30.

Suhad remembers that night.

"I started to lose hope that Rami would be found alive. I knew Rami and his faith, and I was sure he would not do what they asked him to do if he was not convinced that it would please the Lord. I felt that they would not release him because he would tell what had happened and appear a hero. On the other hand, I tried to convince myself that, no, that would not happen. They are human beings. They might beat him, but they would not kill him.

"Doubts came again to my mind that people in Gaza were tough and hard on each other during the army coup. When Hamas took over the PA in Gaza, many people were killed, people from the same Islamic faith, horrible stories. So, if they were that tough on each other, why wouldn't they be even harder on Rami because of his different faith? I put my cellphone beside me, waiting to hear any news at any time.

"Early in the morning, the landline phone rang. I jumped out of bed and answered it. The sad voice of one of the team members said they had found Rami's body.

"At first, I could not imagine that something wrong had happened.

"Is he okay?" I asked him.

"'No,' he said, 'he is dead!'

"I shouted, 'Noooo! Are you sure it was his body? Did you see him? Maybe another one!'

"'No,' he insisted, 'it is Rami.'

"Hanna was still sleeping in the other room. I tried to wake him without waking the girls but was out of control, crying, screaming. I felt chills inside and outside of me, imagining his young wife who is now a widow. What shall we tell her? How can we talk to her? What to say . . . what to do . . ."

I had been asleep only a couple of hours and awoke confused and disoriented.

They had found Rami's body.

I jumped out of bed, but I didn't know where to go or what to do. Who had done this? Why? What will I say to Pauline?

"It was not 6 am yet," Suhad recalls, "and I did not know who to call and what to say. I tried hard to avoid calling Labib Madanat, the director of the Palestinian Bible Society, because of a health issue at that time, but I could not reach any of his staff members because it was Sunday. So I decided to call him, not wanting the Bible Society people to hear the news from other sources. Of course, he knew about the kidnapping the day before. As soon as the telephone rang, he answered.

"After I said they found the body and he was killed, I kept crying.

"On the other side, Labib was just saying, 'Ohhh, Jesus! Ohhh, Jesus!'

"Hanna took the phone from me, because I was not able to say any other word.

"On the same day, Labib tried to get permission to come to Gaza to attend Rami's funeral ceremony. God gave him authority, and he arrived at the church right on time. When I saw him, I could not control myself. I ran to him like a little girl who found her dad and cried, 'They killed him! They killed him!'

"With his caring heart and spirit, he quoted Matthew 10:28: 'Do not be afraid of those who will kill the body.'

"Rami was a rock, and I believe that his captors could not shake his faith and could see no other choice but to kill his body and hide his victory."

The funeral was at the Greek Orthodox church. Rami was buried in their cemetery. Some reports said he had been stabbed and tortured, but we had seen his body and he had been shot twice, once in the side and once in the back of his head.

Suhad was terrified after Rami's murder.

"As director of the Bible Society, I was responsible for the whole team, as well as being a pastor's wife. It was a huge responsibility. In addition, members of the Greek Orthodox church in Gaza blamed us for Rami's death, which made it very difficult for us to support his family and other team members. I was not able to close my eyes to sleep at night. Every night, I imagined someone following Rami and trying to kill him.

"Fear got in me more and more. Whose turn is next? Other team members? My husband? Maybe our kids. What would happen if they hurt me? What am I going to tell my daughters?

"I was worried to let Hanna go outside our home, and I didn't want him to leave me alone. I kept checking to see if anyone was watching us through the windows, going outside, checking if anyone was watching or following us. Food stuck in my throat.

"The day after the funeral, we did not allow Joyce to go to kindergarten. The same with other team member's kids. But, as parents, we started to think that if we allow the fear to get inside us, our kids will get it too. So the next day, we asked a taxi driver we knew well to pick up our kids from home and return them after school. We gave him instructions not to stop for anyone, stay in his car while the kids were with him, be careful and watch if anyone is following him.

"I remember the first day Joyce went to school. I ran downstairs, waiting at the outside door for her to return, holding my phone, watching the time. She was late. One. Two. Three minutes. It seemed like an hour. I started to worry more. Then, the taxi pulled up.

"'Don't worry,' the taxi driver told me, 'everything is okay. All the kids are okay.'"

In the beginning, there was a lot of fear and anxiety among church leaders and their families. At the same time, some people in the Christian community blamed us for the persecution. They thought we were proselytizing Muslims.

"You are the one who killed him!" a Christian mourner accused me after Rami's funeral.

"You are traders of blood," charged another.

These were painful accusations, but I was amazed at the peace in my heart that only the Lord could give. In both cases, I sincerely asked that God would forgive and bless them. We were not proselytizing. We were merely reaching out to those in need, both Christian and Muslim, with Christ's unconditional love.

At that time, we seemed to be the only target of the persecution. Unfortunately, it eventually targeted the Catholics and Greek Orthodox.[46]

---

[46] Abu Toameh, Khaled, "Who Will Save the Christians in the Gaza Strip?" Gatestone Institute International Policy Council, 20 July 2012: www.gatestoneinstitute.org, retrieved 062418.

*"[A]t least five Christians have been kidnapped and
forced to convert to Islam in recent weeks," said a
news report five years later. "If anyone has good
reason to fear for his life it is Archbishop Alexios,
head of the Greek Church in the Gaza Strip, who is
spearheading the protests against persecution of
Christians and forced conversions."*

Soon, the militants who killed Rami went after another
team member. A couple of them came to his house. He wasn't
home, but somebody said they saw two young men carrying
something in a bag.

I called Zahar and told him what was happening, He
was very surprised. He said these killers are going to cause a
lot of trouble for them, and he asked me if I wanted him to
protect me and our team members. I didn't think it would be
wise to have Hamas policemen protecting us in our own land,
in a place we call home, so I said no.

With Rami's death, there was talk of leaving. I didn't think
it was necessary until one night a member of our leadership
team called.

"There are eyes on you and on us, and people following
us," he said. "They know everything about us and what we do."

So we, along with seven other leadership families, began
the process of getting permission to leave Gaza. We didn't take
much with us, because we didn't expect to be gone for more
than a couple of weeks.

This was one of the most difficult decisions I have had to make in my life. I was torn among my roles as shepherd, husband and father. Some thought I had betrayed my congregation, but I felt I needed to take care of my family. At the same time, I told Suhad that this was not the way I ever imagined to leave Gaza. This is why I continue today to go back and forth to minister in Gaza, despite the growing risks.

By now, my brother, one of my sisters and our mother had died. And God helped me find special help for my two surviving sisters.

"I remember when we left Gaza," Suhad recalls. "I asked Hanna what shall I take with me. He said, 'just a few things. We will not be long. Just a couple of weeks and we will be back home.'

"Hmmmm, we had just returned from a summer trip to the US, and I had clothing for the girls for the next summer (got it on a huge sale, which we do not experience back home). So I decided to roll these things up and put them in a suitcase. We took just two suitcases for the whole family!"

A few weeks after we buried Rami, we left for Beit Jala in the West Bank.

8. Flight

NOTHING I HAD EXPERIENCED was more difficult or painful for me than leaving Gaza. When we didn't return after a couple of weeks, some people accused us of cowardice and abandoning our responsibilities, charges that cut deeply.

If someone asks, "What are these wounds on your body?" they will answer, "The wounds I was given at the house of my friends."[47]

I had watched Suhad lose weight and waste away in front of my eyes. I watched her anguish over decisions as director of the Bible Society in Gaza, reopening the bookstore after the bomb blast in opposition to the will of the building owner. None of us suspected that anyone would be killed.

We do well to settle our life priorities before we find ourselves in the fire, where it is especially hard to hear God's voice. I had determined that my priorities were God first, family second and ministry third. Family should come before ministry, unless we have clear direction from God otherwise. It breaks my heart to see so many damaged families of pastors and evangelists who put their ministry first.

When Suhad, Joyce (almost 3), Jolene (16 months) and I arrived in Beit Jala, we stayed at the guesthouse at Talitha Kumi, a German international school. They provided us with one room per family. And counselors helped us process everything that had happened. Churches throughout the West Bank and Jerusalem received and embraced us as heroes and helped us in every way possible. After two weeks, we were ready to move to the house of Suhad's uncle in Beit Sahour.

---

[47] Zechariah 13:6.

Late one evening, as we were taking a taxi there, nearly half a dozen IDF soldiers stopped us at gunpoint and asked for our papers.

Suhad was terrified and quickly started to cover the girls' eyes, afraid they were about to witness a horrible sight. At the same time, she thrashed around in her bag in search of our permissions, finally finding all except mine. Desperately, she continued to look for several minutes more and finally found it. For Suhad, though, it felt like hours.

They allowed us to go to Beit Sahour, where we stayed for a few months, then rented a place in a pastor's house for seven more.

One day, in the midst of our time in the West Bank, Suhad told me she was ready to return to Gaza. Wow! What a courageous woman!

We started to contact the people who usually help us to get permissions and visas. But nothing worked out, and it was clear to us that God had shut the door to Gaza.

Only one door remained open. We headed for America, despite accusations that we were scared and running away.

"Moving out of our home in Gaza and being in three different places in the West Bank was not easy," Suhad recalls. "The pressure on us was great, even in the West Bank. Some people could not understand what we were passing through, what pressures and fears. They were only concerned about who we left in charge. Some even asked us when we are going back. At that time, we were not ready even to hear it, much less to do it.

"After a few months, we started to feel it was time to go home. The situation was better, and we had taken time to mourn and be refreshed. We tried, but my visa had expired again, and I was not able to renew it. Even the person who had helped me before had disappeared. So, with an expired visa, I couldn't cross back to Gaza. Not only that, but I would be at risk of deportation from the West Bank to Jordan. So it was just God's timing for everything. When I left Gaza, I had a valid visa, which would expire in a couple of weeks or so."

Scripture has a great deal to say about fleeing. God told Lot and his family to flee Sodom.

"Flee for your lives! Don't look back, and don't stop anywhere in the plain! Flee to the mountains or you will be swept away![48]

God established cities of refuge to which those who killed without intending to could flee.

Then the Lord said to Moses: "Speak to the Israelites and say to them: 'When you cross the Jordan into Canaan, select some towns to be your cities of refuge, to which a person who has killed someone accidentally may flee. They will be places of refuge from the avenger, so that anyone accused of murder may not die before they stand trial before the assembly.[49]

David, the man after God's own heart, a courageous warrior who slayed tens of thousands of armed soldiers, fled Absalom.

---

[48] Genesis 19:17.
[49] Numbers 35:9-12.

A messenger came and told David, "The hearts of the people of Israel are with Absalom." Then David said to all his officials who were with him in Jerusalem, "Come! We must flee, or none of us will escape from Absalom. We must leave immediately, or he will move quickly to overtake us and bring ruin on us and put the city to the sword." [50]

God told Joseph to flee Bethlehem with his family.

When they had gone, an angel of the Lord appeared to Joseph in a dream. "Get up," he said, "take the child and his mother and escape to Egypt. Stay there until I tell you, for Herod is going to search for the child to kill him." [51]

The first Christians fled Jerusalem after Stephen was martyred.

On that day a great persecution broke out against the church in Jerusalem, and all except the apostles were scattered throughout Judea and Samaria. [52]

When the Jews plotted to kill Saul, he fled Damascus to Tarsus.

After many days had gone by, there was a conspiracy

---

[50] 2 Samuel 15:13-14.
[51] Matthew 2:13.
[52] Acts 8.

among the Jews to kill him, but Saul learned of their plan. Day and night they kept close watch on the city gates in order to kill him. But his followers took him by night and lowered him in a basket through an opening in the wall. [53]

Jesus fled when the Jews tried to kill Him.

"Very truly I tell you," Jesus answered, "before Abraham was born, I am!" At this, they picked up stones to stone him, but Jesus hid himself, slipping away from the temple grounds. [54]

"When they persecute you in one town," he said, "flee to another. Truly I tell you, you will not finish going through the towns of Israel before the Son of Man comes." [55]

Our faith is tested in the dark hours, not when everything is going right. And God uses every test to make us stronger.

Consider it pure joy, my brothers and sisters, whenever you face trials of many kinds, because you know that the testing of your faith produces perseverance. Let perseverance finish its work so that you may be mature and complete, not lacking anything. [56]

The word "testing" in the time of James was used when examining a coin to see if it was real or counterfeit.

This is the time when our faith will be tested, not when everything is going fine, but in the most difficult

---

[53] Acts 9:23-25.
[54] John 8:58-59.
[55] Matthew 10:23.
[56] James 1:2-4.

times of our life, in the darkest hours. Then, our faith will be revealed as genuine or fake. If we pass the test and our faith is real, we gain the virtue of perseverance, which will help shape us into the person God has intended us to be.

We may never know why Rami was chosen instead of other leaders who were much more active in outreach. It could have been any of us. Personally, I think Rami was better prepared than anyone on the team. God knew he could bear up under the pressure.

In the time of persecution in Gaza, the secret police told us they could not protect us. You have to take care of yourselves, they said. So, when I said the Lord is my shepherd or refuge or shelter, I meant it literally, because the time had come when nobody would help us, when we needed to lean on the Lord.

What do you do when you feel your life and the lives of your family members are on the line? You start to ask the big questions. What is life all about? Why am I here? Where am I going? What are my priorities?

When I go through tough times, I remind myself, Hanna, which is bigger, your problem or your God? Your faith or the challenge you are facing? If I make my problem bigger than my God, this is disaster. But if I see things in the right perspective, things will be fine. To know who my God is and who I am as His child enables me to arrange my priorities correctly.

In the toughest time in my life, where fear and anxiety were very high, the Lord said, "Hanna, the most important thing for you is to be in the midst of my will."

Even if I am in one of the most difficult places in the world, like Gaza, it will become the best and safest place for me. But if I am out of His will, even America will be the worst place for me.

The Lord also taught us the cost of discipleship. In

any translation, you will find the word "disciple" many more times than the word "Christian." While it is an honor to be called Christian, God's heart is for us all to become disciples. Many want to follow Christ, but few are willing to pay the price of actually doing it.

During the persecution, the Lord spoke to my heart, saying, "Hanna, do you want to follow me from afar, or are you willing to go all the way to the cross?"

Pauline said Rami could have come home if he had wanted to, if he converted to Islam. But she knew how much he loved his two-and-a-half-year-old son, George. And she knew that her husband could not raise their son in a lie. After his death, Pauline continued to thank God that her husband did not come back to them a Muslim.

She knew that, in his darkest hour, Rami remembered the word of Jesus, that if you confess me before people, He will confess you before His Father. She knew that Rami kept his eyes on the Lord and was willing to pay the ultimate price for the truth.

My prayer is, "Lord, if it's Your will that one day I walk the same road as Rami, that I too would not be hesitant or withdraw or compromise my faith but, like him, I would keep my eyes on You."

After Rami's death, I felt that the Lord took me to a new level of how to love and relate to my brothers and sisters. He reminded me that his children around the world are laying down their lives for what they believe, while others are fighting among themselves about silly things, rather than praying for help, rather than using the most powerful tool he has given us—the tool of love.

"During this time of pain and denial," Pauline recalls, "I only saw myself and my selfishness. It was a journey that I went through on my own, in a closed circle, a circle I wanted no one to be a part of, except for Satan who made his way into it without me knowing. I lived a life of misery, suffering, hatred, self-pity, jealousy and anger towards God. I convinced myself that my loving Father had forgotten and neglected me.

"When I finally opened the doors, I understood the greatness of what I had experienced. I hadn't realized what it really meant to be a martyr for Christ. I hadn't realized the meaning of sacrificing my whole life for God. I had only looked at myself and my needs and hadn't seen the glory in Rami's sacrificing his life.

"Finally, I saw God's plan in my life. I was able to see a glimpse of hope. In the midst of all the darkness, Jesus lights the way. He comforts me and wipes away every tear. He gives me hope, so that I may live in His unfailing love that gives me strength to forgive those who have wronged me."

I will never forgot what Pauline said on the first anniversary of Rami's martyrdom.

"May the people who murdered Rami come to know the Lord. This is my revenge."

A few years later, she appeared on Arabic Christian satellite TV, watched by millions of Muslims all over the Middle East. She said she had forgiven the killers of her husband because of what Jesus did on Calvary.

Forgiveness has become more and more common in the Middle East, especially in the past fifteen years. It fills the hearts of Egyptian families whose children were slaughtered by ISIS on the beaches of Libya, those who lost loved ones when terrorists blew up their churches and Iraqi families whose loved ones were murdered by Islamic terrorists.

The voice of forgiveness has become much louder than the noise of murders and much more powerful than the sword. When all these people offer forgiveness to those who murdered their husbands, wives, parents and children, militants all over the Middle East have to ask themselves what—or Who—gives them this power?

As a result, many have come to know personally this amazing Lord.

9. Forgiveness

OFFENSES COME in every size and shape, from slights and insults to cruel betrayals and devastating losses. Healing and freedom, on the other hand, come through forgiveness. I have seen signs in shops in America that read:

You Break It—You Bought It!

Offense and forgiveness are like that. An offense breaks something. Forgiveness pays for the damage and settles the account. If I borrow money from you and then can't or won't pay you back, you suffer a financial injury, an offense. The debt remains until somebody pays it. By forgiving me, you pay the debt I owe, closing the account.

Sometimes, we think we have forgiven when we really haven't. Yes, you say, "I forgive your debt." But what if one day I hand you the money I borrowed? If you accept it, that shows you never forgave the debt, because the account remained open. If the account had been truly closed, you couldn't accept the money. This is why we often continue to suffer from an offense even after we think we've forgiven the offender.

The problem for most people is that they never even try to forgive. Some people enjoy self-righteousness, having persuaded themselves that being wounded makes them superior to the offender. Some place too high a value on themselves, as if offending them was like the commission of the unpardonable sin. Others think their
refusal to forgive hurts the offender. But it really only hurts the victim and ensures that he will remain a victim for the rest of his life. Unforgiveness keeps wounds from healing.

"There is an enormous physical burden to being hurt and disappointed," says Karen Swartz, M.D., director of the Mood Disorders Adult Consultation Clinic at The Johns Hopkins Hospital. Chronic anger puts you into fight-or-flight mode, which results in numerous changes in heart rate, blood pressure and immune response. Those changes, then, increase the risk of depression, heart disease and diabetes, among other conditions. Forgiveness, however, calms stress levels, leading to improved health.[57]

Some people refuse to forgive because they don't understand what forgiveness is *not*. Forgiveness is not excusing. There was no excuse for murdering Rami. The people who killed him were deceived by religion.

[T]he time is coming when anyone who kills you will think they are offering a service to God. They will do such things because they have not known the Father or me. I have told you this, so that when their time comes you will remember that I warned you about them.[58]

Forgiveness is not forgetting. A drunk driver hits my car and I lose my leg. While I forgive him by requiring nothing from him in recompense for my leg and renouncing any claim to revenge, I am unlikely to forget his negligence.

Forgiveness is not reconciliation. Rather it is a prerequisite to reconciliation.

---

[57] "Forgiveness: Your Health Depends on It," Retrieved 062018 from http://www.hopkinsmedicine.org.
[58] John 16:2-4.

An Israeli family whose mother was killed by a militant Palestinian can forgive the killer without having to become friends with him, as can a Palestinian father whose young daughter was shot by an IDF soldier during a public demonstration.

Forgiveness also does not mean that trust is restored. It could, however, bring about a two-state solution with peaceful coexistence for Israel and Palestine. In fact, forgiveness is the only hope for a lasting peace. Everything else—negotiation, military occupation, terrorism, siege and sanction—has failed.

The body of Christ should be an example to the world of the power and glory of forgiveness, because we, above all people, know how much our sins hurt God and how much He has forgiven us.

Sadly, we are more like the servant whose master forgave him ten thousand talents who then refused to forgive the hundred silver coins[59] owed him by a fellow servant.

> *Then the master called the servant in. "You wicked servant," he said. "I cancelled all that debt of yours because you begged me to. Shouldn't you have had mercy on your fellow servant just as I had on you?" In anger his master handed him over to the jailers to be tortured, until he should pay back all he owed. This is how my heavenly Father will treat each of you unless you forgive*
> *your brother or sister from your heart.*[60]

---

[59] A silver coin (denarius) was the usual daily wage of a day laborer (NIV footnote) or about $62 today.
[60] Matthew 18:32-35.

Some people believe that forgiveness is impossible between Palestinian and Israeli. They think the offenses are too horrible and too many and cut too deeply. But Dr. Salim Munayer and his staff at *Musalaha*[61] in East Jerusalem have been successfully reconciling Palestinian Christians and Messianic Jews for more than a quarter of a century by helping them to see one another as people, with very much in common, rather than as enemies with irreconcilable differences and outstanding debts.

Forgiveness is also not a feeling. If I break a piece of china, I don't have to hug the clerk when I pay for it.

Countless family members throughout the world have forgiven those who have taken the lives of loved ones without experiencing affection for the offender. When I decide to forgive, I know from God's word that it is the right thing to do, in spite of my confused or mixed emotions.

Forgiveness requires neither repentance nor a response from the offender. Clearly, the offender does not have to ask for forgiveness, be sorry for his offense or even to stop offending in order for us to forgive him. Returning to Jesus' parable of the unmerciful servant:

> *Then Peter came to Jesus and asked, "Lord, how many times shall I forgive my brother or sister who sins against me? Up to seven times?" Jesus answered, "I tell you, not seven times, but seventy times seven"*[62]

So, God says that even if someone offends me 490 times, I must forgive him every time, with or without repentance, just as He does with us.

---

[61] The Arabic word for "reconciliation."
[62] Matthew 18:21-22.

But God demonstrates his own love for us in this:
While we were still sinners, Christ died for us.[63]

In fact, the offender does not have to respond at all. If he did, how could we forgive people who have offended us and have died? If forgiveness required a response, we would remain victims forever. Perhaps the most sobering truth about forgiveness is found in Matthew 6:15.

But if you do not forgive others their sins, your Father
will not forgive your sins.

Praying for our enemies is another powerful tool.

You have heard that it was said, "Love your neighbor
and hate your enemy." But I tell you, love your
enemies and pray for those who persecute you, that
you may be children of your Father in heaven.[64]

God created us with logical minds. Blessing and praying for enemies is illogical to our logical mind. So it compensates by rationalizing, which is an "attempt to explain or justify one's own or another's behavior or attitude with logical, plausible reasons, even if these are not true."[65]

In effect, the more we bless and pray for someone we perceive as an enemy, the more our brain tells us he or she must be a friend. Physiologically, we replace old neural paths with new ones. The person connected to our perception of *enemy* becomes reconnected to our perception of *non-enemy* and even *friend*.

---

[63] Romans 5:8.
[64] Matthew 5:43-45.
[65] *The New Oxford American Dictionary*, Edited by Elizabeth J. Jewell and Frank Abate, Oxford University Press, 2001, p. 1413.

Sebastian Seung, a professor of computational neuroscience at Harvard, calls the brain's neuron network a *connectome*, which changes by reweighting, reconnection, rewiring and regeneration.

"Reconnection," he explains, "means creation of an entirely new connection or the elimination of an old one."[66]

The Apostle Paul describes it as being "made new by every revelation that's been given to you."[67]

What about forgiveness on a national or ethnic level? How can the State of Israel or the Palestinian people forgive one another?

Philip Yancey offers an encouraging illustration.

[T]wo peacemakers . . . visited a group of Polish Christians ten years after the end of WW II. "Would you be willing to meet with other Christians from West Germany?" asked the two

peacemakers. "They want to ask forgiveness for what Germany did to Poland during the war and to begin to build a new relationship." At first there was silence. Then one Pole spoke up.

"What you are asking is impossible. Each stone of Warsaw is soaked in Polish blood! We cannot forgive!"

Before the group parted, however, they said the Lord's Prayer together. When they reached the words "forgive us our sins as we forgive . . ." everyone stopped praying. Tension swelled in the room.

---

[66] Sample, Ian, "Sebastian Seung: you are your connectome," *The Guardian*, US Edition, 9 June 2012.

[67] The Passion Translation (TPT).

The Pole who had spoken so vehemently said, "I must say yes to you. I could no more pray the Our Father, I could no longer call myself a Christian, if I refuse to forgive. Humanly speaking, I cannot do it, but God will give us his strength!"

Eighteen months later, the Polish and West German Christians met in Vienna, establishing friendships that continue to this day.[68]

As someone once said, no word in the lexicon of mankind carries greater hope and the greater possibility of terror than the word "as" the two times it appears in the Lord's Prayer.

The Holy Spirit taught us about forgiveness while we were in the fires of persecution. He also taught us the cost of discipleship. While it is an honor for us to be called Christians, the term is mentioned only three times in the entire Bible. But the word "disciple" is mentioned 232 times. Salvation is free. Jesus paid the full, terrible price. But discipleship costs us.

Paul declared, "I have been crucified with Christ; and it is no longer I who live, but Christ lives in me; and the life which I now live in the flesh I live by faith in the Son of God, who loved me and gave Himself up for me."[69] Discipleship means dying to our self-interest.

---

[68] Yancey, Philip. *What's So Amazing about Grace?* Grand Rapids: Zondervan, 1997, 87.
[69] Galatians 2:20.

You were taught, with regard to your former way of life, to put off your old self, which is being corrupted by its deceitful desires; to be made new in the attitude of your minds; and to put on the new self, created to be like God in true righteousness and holiness.[70]

What is more, I consider everything a loss because of the surpassing worth of knowing Christ Jesus my Lord, for whose sake I have lost all things. I consider them garbage, that I may gain Christ and be found in him not having a righteousness of my own that comes from the law, but that which is through faith in Christ—the righteousness that comes from God on the basis of faith. I want to know Christ—yes, to know the power of his resurrection and participation in his sufferings, becoming like him in his death, and so, somehow, attaining to the resurrection from the dead.[71]

"Whoever wants to be my disciple," Jesus said, "must deny themselves and take up their cross daily and follow me. For whoever wants to save their life will lose it, but whoever loses their life for me will save it."[72]

We also become more aware of God's presence in the fires of persecution. Just as our physical senses are more acute when we are in danger, our spiritual senses seem to become sharper and more sensitive to the supernatural. This increased awareness of the presence of the Lord is our joy and strength.

In the 17th century, a lay brother among the Carmelites at Paris, known simply as Brother Lawrence, wrote:

---

[70] Ephesians 4:22-24.
[71] Philippians 3:8-11.
[72] Luke 9:23-24.

I consider myself as the most wretched of men, full of sores and corruption, and who has committed all sorts of crimes against his King. Touched with a sensible regret, I confess to Him all my wickedness, I ask His forgiveness, I abandon myself in His hands that He may do what He pleases with me. The King, full of mercy and goodness, very far from chastising me, embraces me with love, makes me eat at His table, serves me with His own hands, gives me the key of His treasures; He converses and delights Himself with me incessantly, in a thousand and a thousand ways, and treats me in all respects as His favorite. It is thus I consider myself from time to time in His holy presence. . . . If sometimes my thoughts wander from it by necessity or infirmity, I am presently recalled by inward motions so charming and delicious that I am ashamed to mention them.[73]

The fires of persecution also make us more empathic for the suffering of others.

One time, Brother Andrew came and preached in our church in Gaza and showed pictures of blood on the walls of a small church that was attacked in Pakistan.

God moved my heart, and we took up a collection for our brothers and sisters. We sent Brother Andrew back with our gift, and he was surprised that such a small congregation had given so much money. But we related to the suffering of our Pakistani brethren because we are brothers and sisters in Christ as well as in suffering.

---

[73] Lawrence, Brother, *The Practice of the Presence of God: Being Conversations and Letters of Nicholas Herman of Lorraine*, translated from the French, 1958, Fleming H. Revell Company.

Someone said that if you want God to perform a miracle in your life, you have to be willing to need one. Likewise, if you want to experience the Holy Spirit's comfort, you have to be willing to need it.

Pauline shared that some of the hardest times after Rami's death were when two-and-a-half-year-old George asked where his father was. Once, she pulled up Rami's photo on the computer and George ran over and hugged the computer. Another time, after she had received no acceptable answer, her son left the room and went outside. When he came back, he was happy.

"I saw him!" George shouted, "I saw him!"

Pauline wasn't sure what had happened, but she felt that the Lord had intervened in a divine way to comfort her young son.

> *Praise be to the God and Father of our Lord Jesus Christ, the Father of compassion and the God of all comfort, who comforts us in all our troubles, so that we can comfort those in any trouble with the comfort we ourselves receive from God. For just as we share abundantly in the sufferings of Christ, so also our comfort abounds through Christ.*[74]

I have heard that some Western Christians actually pray for persecution in the belief that it will heal the church. But this is not biblical. Persecution does not make a weak church strong or a sick church healthy. The early church was so vibrant that it threatened the status quo of the Roman Empire, exalting a crucified carpenter's Son above its emperor. It also threatened the power and influence of the Scribes and Pharisees who corrupted Israel. Persecution was inevitable. But it didn't *heal* the early church; it *spread* it to the ends of the earth.

---

[74] 2 Corinthians 1:3-5.

In Gaza, some Christians of weak faith give in to fear and intimidation and convert to Islam. But Christians like Rami, whose faith is strong, freely surrender their lives for their faith.

When a church becomes more of an organization than a living organism, it does what is politically expedient to survive, like China's Three-Self Church that has submitted its practices and even its beliefs to government control.

We stayed in Beit Sahour and Beit Jala for about nine months, teaching and preaching and training leaders. One day, I was invited to attend an historical gathering at the Georgia World Congress Center in Atlanta. I told the contact person that I was unable to leave the West Bank because Israel refused to give me permission, even though I was an American citizen.

One day, just a few days before the conference, my cellphone rang, and I was told that President Carter wanted to help me.

The Israelis suddenly arranged everything for me to leave, walking me through the process step by step. When I arrived at the Allenby Bridge in Jericho, it was closed, but they arranged for a special car to take me across to Jordan. On the Jordanian side, some paperwork
was missing, but Passport Control, knowing that I was going to speak at a conference headed by President Carter, was eager to help.

I met President and Mrs. Carter in a tent next to the stage. Before I went to speak, Mrs. Carter told me that her husband had tried hard to get the right connection in Israel to get me out on time. I understood that he had contacted Israeli Defense Minister Ehud Barak.

Twenty thousand pastors and Baptist leaders, representing more than thirty Baptist organizations, laid the groundwork that week for what would become The New Baptist Covenant.

I was humbled to sit on the stage with former US Presidents Bill Clinton and Jimmy Carter and share with the attendees what it was like to be a Palestinian under Occupation and a pastor in Gaza.

"Don't forget about the checkpoints," President Carter reminded me as I rose to speak.

When I finished, the convention gave me a standing ovation, and all I could think of was what an amazing Father I had, who could take a little Palestinian boy from Gaza to a seat beside two American presidents.

After nearly a year in the West Bank, we left for a much-needed sabbatical in Connecticut.

When we arrived, we occasionally heard gunshots, making us understandably nervous and causing some sleepless nights.

"Please take me home," Suhad begged. "This is why we left Gaza."

We learned that the neighborhood a few streets over had been having some trouble with drug traffickers. But it was nothing like Gaza.

During our sabbatical, we stayed at The Overseas Ministries Study Center (OMSC), a block from Yale Divinity School.

Established in 1922 as an apartment complex in Ventnor-by-the-Sea, New Jersey, it was a place where missionaries on furlough could go to recover their health and refresh their spirits before returning to their mission fields. In 1987, it moved to New Haven.

While we were there, I traveled, making American Christians aware of the suffering of their brothers and sisters in Gaza. Also, during this time, Suhad qualified for US citizenship, which meant that her visa problem to enter Gaza became much easier and we could return home to minister to the church we loved.

We still agonized over whether to return to Gaza, but we felt restrained by the Lord. We did not at all feel that we were finished with Gaza, but he had other work for us in Jordan as well.

10. The Conflict

AS A PALESTINIAN, pastoring an evangelical church in the midst of conflict, uprising and hostility, I struggled greatly because of Israeli injustices to my parents, grandparents and everyone else I knew. But I was hesitant to speak out against those injustices because I was afraid I would be cursed by God. Many of the books translated into Arabic at that time were from a dispensationalist perspective that emphasizes unconditional support of the State of Israel as the fulfillment of biblical prophecy.

> *The Lord had said to Abram, "Go from your country, your people and your father's household to the land I will show you. I will make you into a great nation, and I will bless you; I will make your name great, and you will be a blessing. I will bless those who bless you, and whoever curses you I will curse; and all peoples on earth will be blessed through you.*[75]

We were believers, but we were not mature, so we accepted a lot without being able to discern what was true and what was not.

After I came to Fuller Theological Seminary, I began to see a way to balance my faith and identity, to reflect God's love, speak against injustice and yet be reconciled with Jewish believers who also struggle with their faith and identity in relation to their culture.

---

[75] Genesis 12:1-3.

The first issue, in discussing the conflict between Palestine and Israel, is how far back in history we need to go to resolve it. And the answer is no further than the start of the First World War.

In November 1917, British Foreign Secretary Arthur Balfour, a Christian Zionist, wrote a letter to Baron Lionel Walter Rothschild, a prominent Jewish Briton, confirming a government decision to help the Jewish people start their own state in Palestine.

Around the same time, Sir Henry McMahon, British High Commissioner in Egypt, wrote to the Sharif of Mecca, soliciting Arab support in the war against the Ottomans and promising that the Arab countries would be granted independence when the war was over.

Balfour's promise was kept; McMahon's was not. In the opinion of former British Foreign Secretary Sir Edward Grey, it was an impossible promise from the start, and he said so in a speech to the House of Lords in March 1923.

> *I think that we are placed in considerable difficulty by the Balfour Declaration itself. I have not the actual words here, but I think the noble Duke opposite will not find fault with my summary of it. It promised a Zionist home without prejudice to the civil and religious rights of the population of Palestine. A Zionist home, my lords, undoubtedly means or implies a Zionist government over the district in which the home is placed, and if 93 percent of the population of Palestine are Arabs, I do not see how you can establish other than an Arab government, without prejudice to their civil rights. That one sentence alone of the Balfour Declaration seems to me to involve, without overstating the*

case, very great difficulty of fulfillment.[76]

While it was illogical to have a Palestinian majority governed by any but a Palestinian government, the Arabs were not against the Jewish people escaping from the Nazi regime or immigrating to Palestine; only against a Jewish State in Palestine. In a secret memorandum submitted to the British cabinet in 1919, however, Lord Balfour had made it clear that the government had no intention of allowing Arab self-government in Palestine. Fueling the flames were Zionist colonists who flooded into Palestine, supported by British immigration policies. A Quaker author described Zionism:

> *Beginning in the 1860s, there were groups of European Jews who preached the then improbable dream of migration to the Holy Land of Palestine and acted upon it. An imaginative and determined central European journalist, Theodor Herzl, took up the idea and in 1897, at Basle, Switzerland, challenged the first World Zionist Organization to develop a program for creating a Jewish homeland. He suggested how this should be achieved in a pamphlet entitled,* The Jewish State.[77]

When Herzl proposed "the establishment of a

---

[76] Khalidi Walid. *From Haven to Conquest: Readings in Zionism and the Palestine Problem Until 1948.* Washington DC: The Institute for Palestinian Studies, 1987, 219-220.

[77] *Search for Peace in the Middle East,* a study prepared by a working party, initiated by the American Friends Service Committee and Canadian Friends Service Committee, acting in association with the Friends Service Council (London), the Friends World Committee for Consultation and the Friends Peace and International Relations Committee (London), (New York: Fawcett Publication, In., 1970, 14.

Jewish state," he "insisted that its purposes should be political and economic, rather than religious."[78]

Today, the focus has become religious rather than political and economic, arguing divine right instead of humanitarian necessity. The Arab majority in Palestine in 1900 was comfortable with having the Jewish people live with them, until they begin to feel threatened and fearful that they might be pushed out and lose their land. Those fears were confirmed by a controversial study:

> *A retired Indian civil service official and an authority on agricultural economics, Hope Simpson, embarked upon three months of travel-investigation and aerial surveys of landholdings. He then issued a massive 185-page report of his own on October 20, 1930. It was Hope Simpson's conclusion that the land available to Arabs was less than previously had been believed. The Arabs, he said, gradually were being driven off the soil by Jewish land purchases and by the JNF[79] policy of not reselling to Arabs or allowing them employment on Jewish tracts.[80]*

During the years leading up to 1947, the Arabs felt their lives threatened. Their relationship with the British and the Jews deteriorated. Unable to resolve the conflict, the UK handed over the problem to the United Nations.

On November 29, 1947, the General Assembly

---

[78] Penrose, Stephen Bill, *The Palestinian Problem: Retrospect and Prospect* (New York: American Friends of the Middle East, 1957), 4.

[79] Jewish National Fund, founded in 1901 to buy and develop land in Palestine for Jewish settlement.

[80] Said, Edward W., *The Question of Palestine*. New York: Times Books, 1980, 175-176.

passed Resolution 181, terminating the British Mandate and calling for the withdrawal of British troops. As for the land issues, the resolution gave forty-eight percent to the Palestinians and fifty-two percent to the Jewish people, which the Jews wisely accepted. When they won the war in 1967, they gained an additional twenty-two percent.

The Palestinians, however, rejected the forty-eight percent, a decision we regret today as we try to simply recover what was taken in the Six-Day War.

Prior to 1948, most of the land was owned or occupied by Palestinians. The war turned more than 700,000 of them into refugees. About 50,000 displaced Palestinians were Christians. They scattered all over the world. Many came to Gaza. And today, more than half a million Palestinian refugees live in our eight UN refugee camps. Others live in camps in the West Bank, Jordan, Lebanon and Syria.

My purpose in sharing so much detail is to expose the root of the problem, which involves two peoples living in and claiming exclusive right to the same land. I also believe that a solution exists that does not involve bitterness, hatred and violence.

As Christians, we have an important role to play, because God "has committed to us the message of reconciliation. We are therefore Christ's ambassadors, as though God were making His appeal through us."[81]

But what about the five covenants? What of God's eternal promises to the Jewish people?

It is important to closely examine them as well, but through the eyes of Christ, not through the blinders of a single Bible verse.[82] The first covenant was with Noah.

---

[81] 2 Corinthians 5:19-20.
[82] Genesis 12:3.

*I establish my covenant with you: Never again will all
life be destroyed by the waters of a flood; never again
will there be a flood to destroy the earth.*[83]

The second covenant was with Abraham, which begins in
Genesis 12:2 and extends to Isaac and Jacob in Genesis 26. It is
also a universal covenant.

*"All the peoples of the earth will be blessed through
you."*[84] *It was a grant covenant, not a bilateral contract,
so Abraham's disobedience did not prevent God's
fulfillment of the promise.*[85]

We saw this covenant fulfilled through the seed of Christ
in Galatians 3:16, 29. The third was with Israel, referred to as
the Mosaic or Sinai covenant.

*Now if you obey me fully and keep my covenant, then
out of all nations you will be my treasured possession.
Although the whole earth is mine, you will be for me a
kingdom of priests and a holy nation.*[86]

But Israel repeatedly broke its covenant with God and was
not permitted to enter the promised land.

Nevertheless, as surely as I live and as surely as

---

[83] Genesis 9:11.
[84] Genesis 12:3.
[85] Bock, Darrell L., and Craig Blaising. *Progressive Dispensationalism*. Wheaton: Bridgepoint, 1993, 132, 134.
[86] Exodus 19:5-6.

the glory of the Lord fills the whole earth, not one of those who saw my glory and the signs I performed in Egypt and in the wilderness but who disobeyed me and tested me ten times—not one who has treated me with contempt will ever see it.[87]

Though Israel breaks the heart of the covenant[88] by worshiping the golden calf, God does not bring this covenant to an end because of who He is,

The Lord, the Lord, the compassionate and gracious God, slow to anger, abounding in love and faithfulness, maintaining love to thousands, and forgiving wickedness, rebellion and sin.[89]

The fourth covenant is with David, and the fifth is announced through the prophet Jeremiah.

"The days are coming," declares the Lord, "when I will make a new covenant with the people of Israel and with the people of Judah. It will not be like the covenant I made with their ancestors when I took them by the hand to lead them out of Egypt, because they broke my covenant, though I was a husband to them," declares the Lord. This is the covenant I will make with the people of Israel after that time," declares the Lord. "I will put my law in their minds and write it on their hearts. I will be their God, and they will be my people. No longer will they teach their neighbor, or say to one another, 'Know the Lord,' because

---

[87] Numbers 14:21-23.
[88] Exodus 32-34.
[89] Exodus 34:6-7

they will all know me, from the least of them to the greatest," declares the Lord. For I will forgive their wickedness and will remember their sins no more."[90]

Some of the covenants are conditional, like the Mosaic, which depends on the people, as well as on God, to continue the covenant. The Abrahamic, Davidic and the new covenant in Jeremiah are unconditional, depending entirely on God to fulfil His promises.

All form a united and progressive redemptive plan, ultimately fulfilled in Jesus Christ.

By calling this covenant "new," he has made the first one obsolete; and what is obsolete and outdated will soon disappear.[91]

Animal sacrifices have disappeared, fully fulfilled in Christ, our perfect sacrifice. The temple has disappeared, fully fulfilled through the indwelling of the Holy Spirit in God's people. And what of the priests?

"Now this shall be the priests' due from the people, from those who offer a sacrifice, either an ox or a sheep, of which they shall give to the priest the shoulder and the two cheeks and the stomach. You shall give him the first fruits of your grain, your new wine, and your oil, and the first shearing of your sheep. For the Lord your

---

[90] Jeremiah 31:31-34.
[91] Hebrews 8:13.

God has chosen him and his sons from all your tribes,
to stand and serve in the name of the Lord forever"[92]

They are fulfilled in the body of Christ.

But you are a chosen people, a royal priesthood, a
holy nation, God's special possession, that you may
declare the praises of him who called you out of
darkness into his wonderful light.[93]

Regarding covenantal promises concerning "the land," [94] the only times "the land" is mentioned in the New Testament is in telling the history of Israel,[95] rather than validating an eternal claim to a geographical area in the Middle East.

The land promised to Abraham and his descendants in Genesis 15 is restricted to a land area *(erets)* "from the Wadi of Egypt to the great river, the Euphrates,"—little more than a dot on a map compared to the universe *(kosmos)* that is promised to God's people in the new covenant.

I do not deny the existence of a unique Jewish people today. As God has shown his faithfulness to them through His Son, many of them already believe and accept the Messiah and are part of the faithful remnant (Romans 11:5). In the future, there will be some special
concern for the Jewish people, some purpose which God will accomplish (Romans 9:11) through salvation in Christ.

We see the heroes of the faith in Hebrews 11:10 looking to a heavenly kingdom, not an earthly city.

---

[92] Deuteronomy 18:3-5 NASB.
[93] 1 Peter 2:9.
[94] Genesis 17:8.
[95] Acts 7:4-5, 45; 13:19; 17:26.

For he was looking forward to the city with
foundations, whose architect and builder is God.

And, in verse 13, the people considered themselves
strangers on the earth, indicating that not even the planet is
their home.

All these people were still living by faith when they
died. They did not receive the things promised; they
only saw them and welcomed them from a distance,
admitting that they were foreigners and strangers on
earth.

Don Hagner, my New Testament professor at Fuller
Seminary, noted to me an important fact in Romans 4:13.

It was not through the law that Abraham and his
offspring received the promise that he would be heir
of the world, but through the righteousness that comes
by faith.

Usually, when God talks about Abraham, Isaac or Jacob,
He connects them to the land. Here, the offspring of Abraham
are connected with the *kosmos* rather than the land. We see a
shift in language to the big picture of God's ultimate plan, not
on a little ethnic group on a little parcel of land, but rather
God's plan and love for all humanity in Christ. No longer
limited to a single ethnic group, all who believe and accept the
work of Christ on the cross become part of the family of God
and inherit the promises of the new covenant fulfilled in Christ.

Judging by Romans 9-11, I believe that God is not finished with the Jewish people, a "remnant chosen by grace."[96] Thousands of Jews today worship Jesus as the Son of God, and many more will come. The problem with many Christians is that they make the minor major
and the major minor when they cause everything to circulate around Israel. They miss God's ultimate plan for all people.

In his first letter, Peter wrote to Gentile believers.

Peter was the first missionary to go to the Gentiles. After a divine trance he experienced on a rooftop in Joppa, Peter took the keys of the kingdom and opened the door of faith for the Gentiles. He broke the religious limitation that the Gospel was only meant for the Jews. Peter found his way to the house of Cornelius, a Roman Gentile, and he and all his family became followers of Jesus. He continued this mission by writing to Christians living in the Roman regions of northeastern Asia Minor (modern-day Turkey), to encourage them in their suffering, provoke holy living and growth in God, and explain their new birth through Christ's blood.[97]

As we saw earlier, in 1 Peter 2:9-10, the apostle used language, speaking to Gentiles, that was used exclusively in the Old Testament for Israel.

But you are a chosen people, a royal priesthood, a holy nation, God's special possession, that you

---

[96] Romans 11:15.
[97] Simmons, Dr. Brian, 1 Peter, Introduction, *The Passion Translation new Testament with Psalms, Proverbs, and Song of Songs*, p.1049.

may declare the praises of him who called you out of darkness into his wonderful light. Once you were not a people, but now you are the people of God; once you had not received mercy, but now you have received mercy.

The apostle now uses the same language for all and any who believes in Christ and what He did on Calvary, regardless of their ethnicity or background.

I want peace between Palestinians and Israelis. I pray that one side will have the courage to forgive the other and that there will one day be a sovereign Israel and an independent Palestine. But peaceful coexistence, while better than endless conflict, is not the greatest peace. It is still short of reconciliation. A peace greater even than reconciliation between Israel and Palestine is the inheritance of every disciple of Christ.

The peace that Jesus gives is delicious, like lying in a lush green pasture beside a pool of rippling water. His peace refreshes and heals my soul—my thoughts, my will and my emotions. It keeps my conscience clear, like a motorist driving the speed limit, not having to look in the mirror for police cars or ahead for radar.

The peace of Jesus warms me in the chill of danger and death. Christ's peace is like fiery horses and chariots surrounding the enemies that surrounded Elisha. It comforts me in hardship and consoles me in loss. It shames my enemies in front of me and rejuvenates me with the oil of His Spirit. God's peace is more than I can contain. It is the assurance that I am pursued by His goodness and mercy and unfailing love and have a standing invitation to live every day of my life and throughout eternity in the awareness of His sweet presence.[98] No true and lasting peace exists apart from the Prince of Peace.

I am able to find my identity in Christ as a Christian Arab Palestinian and at the same time be faithful to Scripture. I hope my brothers and sisters in the West are able to see the other side of the coin, see the whole picture of the Palestinian conflict. I hope the international community will be able to recognize and to deal with not only the symptoms of the problems but also with the root of them, which is the Israeli occupation.

Even though my family lost a lot of land in 1948 and experienced trauma and humiliation because of this occupation, I am able to forgive Israel because I constantly experience God's forgiveness. I am able to love the Jewish people because I experience my Father's love through His beloved Son, our Lord Jesus Christ.

Long ago, I made up my mind and decided in my heart that I will not allow unforgiveness and bitterness to rule my life, because this is not God's will. And I know that, if I ever do, I will lose His influence and destiny in my life. Nothing is more important in my life than to live for the One who gave His life for me.

Again, I do not believe God is finished with the Jewish people. But we need to see things in the correct perspective, to keep major things major and minor things minor, to see the Old Testament through the lens of the New Testament. All the promises and covenants in the Old Testament are fulfilled in Christ in the New Covenant.[99]

---

[98] Psalm 23. The road through the actual Valley of the Shadow of Death referred to in this Psalm runs from Jerusalem to Jericho. It is narrow and winding, ideal for robbers and murderers to lie in wait for vulnerable travelers.

[99] Matthew 26:28 NKJV.

When I share about the injustices we experienced, I am in no way rejecting the Jewish people. And I pray that all my brothers and sisters open a place in their hearts for the Palestinian people alongside their love for the Jews.

I am always blessed by Jewish believers, especially when we pray together. But if we start to discuss politics, we get into trouble.

I will never forget a time at Lausanne II: International Congress on World Evangelization in Manilla in 1989. I was in a small prayer meeting that included believers from Gaza and the West Bank and Messianic Jews from Israel and the West. When a Palestinian brother prayed, "God, give me enough love to die for my Jewish brother," one of the Jews prayed, "Lord, give me enough love to be willing to die for my Palestinian brother." When politicians say it's impossible for these two people groups to get together, Christ says nothing is impossible through me.

> *[A]t that time you were without Christ, being aliens from the commonwealth of Israel and strangers from the covenants of promise, having no hope and without God in the world.*
>
> *But now in Christ Jesus you who once were far off have been brought near by the blood of Christ. For He Himself is our peace, who has made both one, and has broken down the middle wall of separation . . .* [100]

Jews and Gentiles become one through the Cross of Christ and a living testimony to people everywhere. I pray that people will stop killing one another and find common ground and a practical solution. I believe in a two-state solution which will result in security for Israelis in their home country and a home for Palestinians to in harmony and mutual respect.

---

[100] Ephesians 2:12-14 NKJV.

11. Refugees

WE RETURNED TO JORDAN in December 2009. In addition to supporting Gaza Baptist Church, my role with CM2G had frequently taken me back and forth to Amman, where I taught theology at Jordan Evangelical Theological Seminary (JETS) and ministered with Yousef Hashweh, senior pastor of the Christian & Missionary Alliance Church, to the growing number of Iraqi Christians fleeing ISIS terrorism.

This ministry began back in 1991, after the first Gulf War, when Iraqi refugees started coming to Jordan.

There are three goals for this ministry: to encourage people to come in to hear the Gospel, to disciple new believers and to send out these leaders to Arabic-speaking churches in new countries.

Since they are not allowed to work in Jordan, we meet both their spiritual and physical needs. So far, the Lord has entrusted us with 5,000 people.

In October 2010, I was invited to pastor the Iraqi refugee congregation to whom God connected us through mutual pain and suffering.

Many Iraqi refugees are from nominal Christian backgrounds, and it is wonderful to see them come to experience a personal relationship with the Lord and to grow and mature in their faith through Amose School for Bible study.

By 2014, ISIS controlled more than 34,000 square miles in Iraq and Syria, driving tens of thousands more Iraqis north. At that time, in Gaza, the IDF launched a military operation in response to the kidnapping and murder of three Israeli teenagers by Hamas. For a month-and-a-half, Israeli airstrikes and ground bombardment answered rockets fired into Israel by Hamas. Thousands, mostly Gazans, were killed.

The first fatality in the Christian community was Mrs. Jalila Ayyad. Her son, Jeries, lost both legs and an arm. He used to attend Baptist youth meetings.

One day, one of my neighbors in Gaza City called and said the IDF told him he had to evacuate because it was going to bomb the house of a neighbor who was a Hamas militant. He asked if he and his family could use our home as a shelter. I said yes, of course. Soon, nearly seventy people had taken refuge in our home. The Catholic and Greek Orthodox churches opened their doors to hundreds more.

Day after day, in Amman, I listened to refugees share their heartbreaking stories, comforting them as I could with the comfort the Holy Spirit gave to us and helping them meet their physical needs. Most had fled with what they wore and the little they could carry.

Mardeen (30) lived in the Assyrian homeland in northern Iraq, in a town called Batnaya. He and his younger brother and two married sisters belong to the ancient Chaldean Catholic Church. And because his father is disabled, Mardeen and his family were unable to flee when ISIS invaded his town. [101]

On August 6, 2014, they came to his house, demanding that he renounce his faith and convert to Islam or pay *jizya*, a heavy tax imposed on non-Muslims. When he refused, they beat him and dragged
him off to be tortured.

He was hanged by his feet for days and beaten so
badly that one of his legs needed to be amputated. But Mardeen held fast to his faith. They tried three times to force him to marry Muslim women, but he refused. The torture continued for a month-and-a-half and, on the 46th day, they decided to execute him.

---

[101] All names have been changed for protection.

At the last minute, the leader of the kidnappers received a phone call from a higher authority, and the execution was cancelled.

After that, Mardeen remembers waking up and seeing white walls all around him. He thought he had died and was in heaven. A Catholic nun stood by his bedside and explained that a good Samaritan had found him unconscious and soaked in blood along the side of a road and brought him to the hospital. Miraculously, doctors in Europe were able to save his leg. Now, he is in Jordan waiting to emigrate to another country. Mardeen knows that his life was spared by God, not ISIS.

In the West, compromise and denial are extracted by temptations rather than torture. We compromise truth or morality and misrepresent Christ with ungodly lifestyles and in the way we treat our spouse, parents, children, neighbors or customers.

Mardeen's testimony reminds us that God's grace is always sufficient for us, whether we face ISIS torturers or sweet seductions.

Gamri is an automotive mechanic. In 2004, he lived in Mosul with his family and was engaged to be married to a beautiful Armenian woman named Damrina.

One day, Gamri's brother and sister were shot at because they worked as translators with expatriates. When he heard of the attack, Gamri's father had a heart attack and died.

A week later, two vehicles pulled up suddenly, and armed gunmen kidnapped Gamri. His brother witnessed the abduction and was injured trying to stop them.

The kidnappers, who Gamri believed to be Afghans, took him to a school, then changed locations to a stable where he was held for days.

One day, several vehicles arrived with a leader, an interrogator, a doctor and an executioner. They accused him of being a spy for the Americans and tortured him when he denied it. He showed me a scar where they nearly bit off one of his fingers. If the executioner returned the next day, Gamri was told, he would be killed. If the leader came by himself, he would live.

During the time Gamri was held, the kidnappers brought in other prisoners. They put one man in the room next to his and murdered him shortly after that.

In the morning, the leader came alone and brought food, since Gamri hadn't eaten in four days. They forced him to read a statement in front of a video camera in which he said he was being released because his "investigators" had found nothing wrong.

Finally, he was tied, blindfolded and put into the trunk of a car. About ten minutes later, they pulled him out of the trunk and left him by the road.

The next morning, Gamri fled to Syria with his mother, brother and sister where he and Damrina were married.

Because Damrina is a Jordanian citizen, Gamri and his family came to Amman where they have been able to get some financial help to enable their children to attend school. They hope to emigrate to America.

On October 31, 2010, Daniel, his wife and their infant son were worshiping at the Sayidat al-Nejat Syriac Catholic Church in Baghdad, when six ISIS terrorists burst in and began shooting. Daniel managed to get his family to a room with some other families where they hid for what seemed an eternity. Militants threw bombs into the room, killing one person. Another lost both arms.

Fifty-eight worshipers, priests, policemen and bystanders were killed, and seventy-eight more were wounded or maimed. The terrorists detonated their explosive vests when Iraqi commandos stormed the church five hours later.

Before they could leave, Daniel's wife had to convince the Iraqis that she was two months pregnant. They thought she was wearing an explosive vest. Fortunately, when she went to the hospital, she was told that her baby was safe and healthy, but she still suffers from Posttraumatic Stress Disorder.

Four years later, her father was targeted by Islamic militants because he owned a liquor store. One day, while her father, brother and uncle were driving, militants pulled alongside and opened fire, killing her father and injuring her brother and uncle. Daniel was supposed to be with them, but God preserved him.

Again, her family was persecuted by militants and beaten. When local police arrested them, they thought her family had turned them in.

"If you don't withdraw the case," read a message written in blood on their wall, "we will kill you!"

Daniel and his family have been in Jordan for nearly a year. He cannot work, afford to send his two sons to school or get the back surgery he needs. They tried to emigrate to Australia but were denied.

Ten years ago, driving from Baghdad to Mosul, Haidar was stopped at a checkpoint. He was asked for his identity card, which showed that he was a Christian.

While he was being questioned, he sensed that something was not right. He was waved through and proceeded on his way.

Suddenly, a car with four masked men drove him off the road, pulled him out of the car and forced him into the trunk. Bound and blindfolded, he was locked in a mud-room for animals. The men took his possessions "to keep them safe," saying that his name had come up as someone who was working for the Americans. Of course, he wasn't.

Haidar's kidnappers called his family and demanded $200,000 ransom, threatening to kill him if they didn't pay. They said they didn't have that much money. The kidnappers began to bargain down, until they reached $10,000.

Over the next week, the predominantly Christian community of Bartilla raised the ransom. During his imprisonment and beatings, Haidar received supernatural peace from the Lord, and since his release, he continues to praise his Deliverer.

Three years ago, ISIS bombed an area, and a school teacher named Saya escaped with her family to a nearby church building. Five hundred refugees were packed into a hall that was built to hold a hundred.

When she left, she lived in a room with twenty-five other people. She found her way to Jordan in February 2016, intending to move to Australia to live with her mother and sister. But her application was rejected. Efforts to emigrate to America were also fruitless.

Nevertheless, Saya continues to trust God, who is faithful to all his promises.

In December 2016, we visited families in Erbil, northern Iraq, who had lost everything to ISIS. More than 20,000 people had fled in recent weeks. We were surprised when someone told us that we could visit Qaraqosh, Iraq's largest Christian city, that had just been liberated by government forces. Most of its residents were members of the Syriac Catholic Church and had fled the invasion of August 2014. We had to pass through several Kurdish and Iraqi army checkpoints before we could enter. The town was rubble.

We entered the charred ruins of the Church of the Immaculate Conception, the largest Christian church in Iraq, in which, thanks to combined armies, Christians were recently able to celebrate the first Mass in two years.

We shared with them the MP3 New Testaments we had brought and helped and encouraged the families as much as we could.

Many of the one thousand Iraqi Christian refugee families that we minister to in Amman are from Qaraqosh. When we got back to Jordan, I stood in front of my congregation and told them I had just come from their hometown, which had recently been liberated. The room exploded with thanksgiving.

The Christian man who took us to Qaraqosh told me that when ISIS came, he refused to leave and stayed with four other Christian men. The jihadists kidnapped them, locked them in a room and called his father, a high-ranking Iraqi officer, demanding half a million dollars.

"Take our farm," his father told them. "It's worth more than a million dollars."

"We already have that," they said. "It belongs to the Islamic State. If you want your son back, you have to pay."

The man had concealed a cellphone and was able to call his father. "Son," he told him, "if you are able to flee, flee."

They were held captive for nearly a month. One day, during Ramadan, the jihadists came in and said they were going to get the captives some food. After they left, the men looked around and saw no one, so they broke down the door and crawled for forty-five minutes until they reached a Kurdish Peshmerga fighter checkpoint. This was how God spared their lives.

Since then, he and 500 other men organized a Christian militia, afraid it might happen again.

In Amman today, we minister to 5,000 Iraqi refugees. We support a team of seven leaders who help us meet the physical, emotional and spiritual needs of these families. We also partner with doctors, nurses and an eyeglasses ministry, in addition to helping to provide food and medicine and emergency expenses like rent and other necessities.

Because government labor restrictions for non-Jordanian workers are so strict, few Iraqi refugees, who arrive with virtually nothing, can meet them. So we teach women to make quilts that we sell in the United States, enabling them to buy more material and provide a small revenue stream to help support their families.

Because many of the parents cannot afford to send their children to school, we opened a school for them with our partners—Canon Andrew White, known as the "Vicar of Baghdad" and president of the Foundation for Relief and Reconciliation in the Middle East, along with Father Khalil of St. Mary's Church.

Several hundred students, ages five to fourteen, attend classes in the afternoon.

As in Gaza, our ministry is not limited to Christians. We partner with Global Hope Network International to serve a growing population of Syrian refugees who have fled ISIS and the war there.

We invite them to church, share the message of salvation, feed them and help them satisfy their material needs. Unlike their Iraqi counterparts, Syrian refugees are able to obtain work permits under the Jordan Compact.[102]

Nevertheless, eighty percent of Syrian refugees in Jordan live below the poverty line; more than half are children.

---

[102] In February 2016, a refugee compact known as the Jordan Compact was signed to turn "the Syrian refugee crisis into a development opportunity" for Jordan by shifting the focus from short-term humanitarian aid to education, growth, investment and job creation, both for Jordanians and for Syrian refugees." (Government of Jordan). In return for billions of dollars in grants and loans and preferential trade agreements with the European Union (EU), Jordan committed to improving access to education and legal employment for more than 650,000 Syrian refugees.

One is a single mother with three children who had been abused by her husband. Single parenting is difficult enough. Magnify that by the horrors of the anarchy in Syria and the terror of a desperate escape. But I thank our Father that she no longer has to struggle alone. During our visit, we were blessed to realize that she had opened her heart to the Lord for the first time and had begun a new life in His kingdom.

One of the non-Christian families includes five daughters, ranging in age from nine to twenty. They fled Aleppo seven years ago, fearing that the girls would be kidnapped and raped by ISIS militants.

The father is disabled, barely able to walk. When I met him, he was six months behind in his rent, though it is only $315 a month for a very simple house. He could not afford to send his daughters to school.

I sat with them, listened to their story and shared the truth and hope of God's Word. I had the privilege of praying for them and helping them with food and rent, followed up by Global Hope staff.

The father recently attended a church service for the first time. Thank God, he, his wife and daughter have all received Christ into their lives!

On August 4, 2006, seven cars pulled up outside a pharmacy in Mosel. Inside each car were four masked men who went inside, beat the pharmacist and kidnapped him. The kidnappers demanded $100,000 from Saleh's family, eventually settling for half. After the family paid the ransom, however, Saleh's wife received a phone call. They had already murdered her husband.

"Why would you kill him!" Anya shouted.

"He was a Christian infidel," was all they said.

Saleh left behind two daughters, one and two years old. Anya believes that the Muslim man hired by Saleh to help him in the pharmacy was involved with the kidnappers.

According to news reports, the ISIS threat is over.

ISIS has been defeated in Iraq and Syria. The caliphate declared in 2014, which was once the size of Great Britain, is no more. Its de facto capitals, Mosul in Iraq and Raqqa in Syria, were captured after long and bloody sieges in the second half of 2017. Could this happen again? People in Baghdad are pleased that ISIS has

been defeated on the battlefield but wary of celebrating victory too early and nervous that ISIS may not be quite as dead as its leaders claim. The caliphate may have been destroyed but the caliph, Mohammed Baqr al-Baghdadi, is still alive. After the loss of Mosul, ISIS did not make a last stand in any of its remaining strongholds, such as Tal Afar and Hawaija; likewise in Syria, after the fall of Raqqa, it did not fight to the last man in Deir Ezzor, acting as if it was determined to preserve some of its combat strength.[103]

In the meantime, hundreds of thousands of Iraqi and Syrian families still suffer as refugees. Many lost everything. Some are too traumatized to go back. Some are afraid ISIS will return. Those who were able have moved on to other countries.

---

[103] Cockburn, Patrick, "Preview 2018: After a string of defeats in Iraq and Syria what 2018 means for Isis," *Independent*, 1 January 2018, Retrieved 062218.

The world is changing faster and faster. I don't know what lies ahead for me in the Lord. I don't imagine any of us do.

We returned to Connecticut in 2016 when it became clear that our daughter, Joyce, needed special support in school which was unavailable in Jordan. This was yet another time when I was torn between being a pastor and a father.

I continue to travel to Gaza at least three times a year with humanitarian relief and encouragement for the Christian families that remain, as well as reaching out with Christ's love to their Muslim neighbors. Most mission trips include time in Amman ministering to our leadership team and our Iraqi and Syrian refugee families.

While people who do not know Jesus Christ are driven by events and circumstances, we who know Him are led by His Spirit. While those who reject Him stumble through life alone, we are always in His presence. In a world of absentee fathers, our Father is always faithful. Ours is not a world writhing with hatred, cruelty and violence; ours is a kingdom ruled by the God who is Love. We are affected by the former, protected by the latter.

Like the Apostle Paul, we have been crucified with Christ and we no longer live, but Christ lives in each of us. The life we now live in the body, we live by faith in the Son of God, who loves us and gave himself for us.

Have you decided how you will live your life?

This is one of the main questions the Lord put into my heart while we were going through the fires of persecution. What kind of legacy do you want to leave behind?

Rami was two weeks away from turning thirty, but he left behind a rich legacy of faith, faithfulness and determined living without compromise, even at the cost of his life. None of us wants our life to be wasted. I love what Paul said in 2 Timothy 4:6-7.

For I am already being poured out like a drink offering, and the time for my departure is near. I have fought the good fight, I have finished the race, I have kept the faith.

This was the last thing he ever wrote, probably a couple of months before he was murdered by Nero. Paul had fought the good fight. He knew what he had lived
for. He did not waste his energy in valueless things. He had finished the race. Many start out with great enthusiasm to live for God, but few finish in a way that is pleasing to him. Many leaders in the Bible start in a way that is honoring to God but end very sadly. Paul kept the faith. He not only wrote and believed sound doctrine, he lived it day after day, through joy and through suffering.

Since none of us knows the length of time we've been given, we do well to live day to day, not for ourselves but for the one who gave his life for us.

About the Author

Born in Gaza City in 1960, Hanna Massad served as pastor of Gaza Baptist Church, the only Evangelical church amidst nearly two million Muslims, and is the founder and president of Christian Mission to Gaza (CM2G).

Hanna and his family were forced to flee Gaza after the Bible Society bookstore was bombed and one of their leaders was murdered by jihadist militants.

Through CM2G, Hanna continues to minister to Christian families and their Muslim neighbors in Gaza, training leaders, teaching, preaching and providing humanitarian aid. In Jordan, he serves 1,000 Iraqi refugee families, along with Muslim refugees from Syria.

Hanna and his wife, Suhad, live in Connecticut with their daughters, Joyce and Jolene.

For more information, go to www.cm2g.org

Photos

From left: Renei, Mai, Mimi (Hanna's mother), Salem, Hanna, George
(Hanna's father), and Rita.

Suhad's parents, Banayot and Elaine Salsa'a,
three weeks before her mother's death.

135

Suhad, Jolene and Hanna
(seated) Anita Brandow holding Joyce.

Exterior of the original Gaza Baptist Church.

Gaza Baptist Church, new building

AWANA Christmas celebration in the new church, 2006.

Muslims in Gaza stand alongside Christians following the
second bombing of the Bible Society bookstore.

Second bombing of the bookstore.

Bullet hole in the window of Gaza Baptist Church.

(From left) George, Samah, Resam and Pauline Ayyad, with photo of Rami.

[Left front] Suhad and Hanna, with the Iraqi refugee congregation in Jordan.

Joyce, Hanna, Suhad and Jolene Massad.

Hanna & Suhad Massad wearing Bedouin clothes

US President Jimmy Carter, US President Bill Clinton and Dr. Hanna Massad
at the Georgia World Congress Center in Atlanta, February 2008.